GLIMPSES OF AN INVISIBLE GOD

Experiencing God in the Everyday Moments of Life

RACINE, WI

Glimpses of an Invisible God
ISBN: 978-1-970103-94-6 - *Paperback*
ISBN: 978-1-970103-95-3 - *Hardcover*
ISBN: 978-1-970103-48-9 - *Ebook*

Copyright © 2022 by Honor Books
Racine, WI

Cover design by Faille Schmitz.
Manuscript written by Vicki Kuyper and Stephen Parolini.

INTRODUCTION

More than ever before, people are searching—longing for a deeper relationship with God. Most have no problem recognizing His distinguished hand in the bright hues of the rainbow, the magnificent grandeur of the night sky, or the breathtaking vistas of the Grand Canyon. But many of these seekers are hoping for more. *Is He present in the routine moments of my everyday life?* they wonder.

If you have been asking that question, *Glimpses of an Invisible God* is just for you. As you move through its pages, you will enjoy the little stories about people just like you, people who discover that God is really there for them. We have supplied scriptures for each story to guide your reading. Also, you will have an opportunity to learn what can happen when God enters into both the great and small details of your life.

We know you will be blessed as you discover the depth of God's love for you and His commitment to walk with you moment by moment.

Hear my prayer, O Lord; listen to my cry for mercy.

PSALM 86:6 NIV

O Lord, the God who saves me, day and night I cry out before you. May my prayer come before you; turn your ear to my cry.

PSALM 88:1-2 NIV

Pray in the Spirit on all occasions with all kinds of prayers and requests. With this in mind, be alert and alway; keep on praying for all the saints.

EPHESIANS 6:18 NIV

THE BATTLEFIELD OF LIFE

L auren had heard the neighborhood gossip. She knew Sarah was caught in a lie, and blaming Lauren just happened to provide her a way out. At first, Lauren had gone to her and tried to set things straight, but Sarah had just exploded with angry words of denial.

Lauren wanted to fight back, to defend herself. But when she took a few minutes to talk to God, she felt Him whisper, "Wait." Lauren still struggled. She bit her tongue whenever Sarah's name came up. But she honored what God had said.

Months went by. Sarah never changed her story, but something changed in Lauren's heart. Whenever Sarah came to mind, Lauren would take a few moments to pray for her. Then, she would commit the whole situation into God's hands one more time. She couldn't see what was behind Sarah's lies, but she knew God could.

Are there relationships you need to leave in God's hands today?

> NO MATTER WHAT BATTLE YOU'RE FACING,
> PRAYER SHOULD BE YOUR WEAPON OF CHOICE.

I will put my trust in Him.

HEBREWS 2:13 NIV

Those who know your name will trust in you, for you, Lord, have never forsaken those who seek you.

PSALM 9:10 NIV

Do not let your hearts be troubled. Trust in God, trust also in me.

JOHN 14:1 NIV

GIFTS OF LOVE

Chris set the mail on the table, unopened. What was the point? It was just more bills. The occasional advertisement only reminded him of what he and his family couldn't afford. Since he'd been laid off six months ago, everything had changed.

As he turned to leave the kitchen, a hand-addressed envelope caught his eye. He tore it open, and a folded sheet of paper fell onto the table. It read simply, "God brought you to mind today." Tucked inside was a money order, enough to pay for rent and then some. Stunned, Chris remembered his disheartened prayer of just an hour before, asking God for help. He now realized that God's answer to his prayer was in the works even before the words crossed his lips.

It wasn't something he did very often. But words of thanks and praise instantly overflowed from his grateful heart.

Remember, it only takes one God moment to change everything.

NEVER BE AFRAID TO TRUST AN UNKNOWN
FUTURE TO A KNOWN GOD.

To the man who pleases him, God gives wisdom, knowledge, and happiness.

ECCLESIASTES 2:26 NIV

A happy heart makes the face cheerful.

PROVERBS 15:13 NIV

Is any one of you in trouble? He should pray. Is anyone happy? Let him sing songs of praise.

JAMES 5:13 NIV

PERFECT TIMING

"I could really get used to a house like this," Bryce said as he stared into the entertainment room practically drooling at its state-of-the-art home theater setup.

"I agree," Lindy replied, eyeing the ornate, winding staircase, the crystal chandelier, and the two-sided fireplace in the entryway.

"It's yours for the small price of—your souls!" The familiar voice came from behind them.

"Caitlyn—what are you doing here?" Bryce asked.

"Visiting a home I could never afford. I want to see how the happy people live."

Bryce pulled a newspaper story from his jacket and handed it to Caitlyn. "The people who lived here were far from happy."

"I don't get it," Caitlyn responded. "How could they not be happy in a place like this?"

Lindy and Bryce knew God had provided an opportunity to talk to their neighbor about true happiness.

What is your description of true happiness? An expensive home? A big bank account? Fame? Ask God to give you His description.

IT IS NOT HOW MUCH WE HAVE, BUT HOW MUCH WE ENJOY THAT MAKES HAPPINESS.

Man's days are determined; you have decreed the number of his months and have set limits he cannot exceed.

JOB 14:5 NIV

It is God who is at work within you both to will and to do for His good pleasure.

PHILIPPIANS 2:13

My times are in your hands.

PSALM 31:15 NIV

LIFE LINES

D r. Jacobs had been in a hospital more times than he could count, but this was the first time in years when he was the one wearing the open-air gown. He knew the symptoms—and the diagnosis. Neither was promising.

He prayed for his own health, just as he had for the health of so many of his patients over the years. It wasn't easy—not being in charge. But he trusted the One who was. Getting to know God over the years made talking to Him on this difficult day much easier. Those few moments with God helped take the fear out of the future and reminded him of the joy of today.

The illness Dr. Jacobs feared never materialized. But he did not regret his day of reckoning. For the first time, he knew his life was squarely in God's hands.

Have you given your life to God? He promises to treat it with the greatest of care.

THERE ARE THREE THINGS THAT ONLY GOD KNOWS: THE BEGINNING OF THINGS, THE CAUSE OF THINGS, AND THE END OF THINGS.

You have made known to me the path of life; you will fill me with joy in your presence, with eternal pleasures at your right hand.

PSALM 16:11 NIV

———————————

As for me, my contentment is not in wealth, but in seeing you; and knowing all is well between us.

PSALM 17:15 TLB

———————————

Set me in your presence forever.

PSALM 41:12 NIV

WALKING A NEW ROAD

mid the party horns, music, and laughter, Helen looked back over the past ten years. Though her coworkers insisted on telling and retelling the story of her first day on the job — and what became known as "The Great Toner Spill Event" — Helen's recollection landed on the day before she started her job.

It was a Sunday, and Helen was sitting where she always sat on Sunday mornings — on a cold, hard pew in church. But this Sunday was different. For the first time in her young life, she really "got it." She understood this "God thing," as she'd referred to it so many times before. And what a change it made! It was a beginning and a direction she never would have anticipated.

As she blew out the candles on the black-frosted, copier-shaped cake, Helen silently thanked God that she'd seen the signpost reading, "This Way."

God wants to be involved in the everyday moments of your life. Will you let Him?

FAITH WEARS EVERYDAY CLOTHES, AND PROVES HERSELF IN LIFE'S ORDINARY SITUATIONS.

I will sing to the Lord, for he has been good to me.

PSALM 13:6 NIV

I'll make a list of God's gracious dealings, all the things God has done that need praising.

ISAIAH 63:7 MSG

I will sing to the Lord as long as I live; I will praise God to my last breath. May He be pleased by all these thoughts about Him; for He is the source of all my joy.

PSALM 104:34 TLB

TRAFFIC JAM

Rush hour traffic only added to Greg's frustration. By the time he arrived at work, he was ready to fight with anyone who got in his way. By lunchtime, he'd relaxed a bit, but all too soon it was time to drive home. Dinner hour with his family was usually far from pleasant, and Greg knew something had to change. So, he started with the dial on his radio.

He had always felt worship songs should be reserved for church. But when a new Christian radio station started up, promising music with a "positive" message, he decided to try it out for a few days. By the end of the week, his absent-minded humming had turned into full-blown singing. Occasionally, drivers stuck in traffic next to him did a double-take. But usually, they just smiled. And Greg found himself smiling back.

Do you need an attitude change at work, at home, on the highway? Maybe you should discover the daily benefits of worship.

WORSHIP RENEWS THE SPIRIT AS SLEEP RENEWS THE BODY.

I know, my God, that you test the heart and are pleased with integrity. All these things have I given willingly and with honest intent.

1 CHRONICLES 29:17 NIV

The man of integrity walks securely.

PROVERBS 10:9 NIV

May integrity and uprightness protect me, because my hope is in you.

PSALM 25:21 NIV

WHEN NO ONE IS LOOKING

A t last count, Amanda had witnessed seventeen acts of what she called "minor deceit" — customers who broke an item and quietly slipped it back into place without reporting the accident (or carelessness) to a store clerk. In fact, in the three years she'd been working at the gift shop, only one customer had honestly stepped forward. That man, Mike, was now her husband.

"Excuse me. I accidentally knocked this figurine off the shelf, and I'd like to pay for it." Those had been his first words to her — and they had sounded golden. Before Mike, Amanda's relationships always ended in disappointment and deception. But he was different; he was a man of integrity.

On their first anniversary he gave her the broken figurine, which had since been carefully glued together to look nearly new. She hadn't noticed before, but the figure looked a lot like her — especially the smile.

How do you handle those minor indiscretions when you think no one is looking?

IMAGE ISN'T EVERYTHING; INTEGRITY IS.

God is the strength of my heart and my portion forever.

PSALM 73:26 NIV

The Lord your God will keep his covenant of love with you, as he swore to your forefathers. He will love you and bless you and increase your numbers.

DEUTERONOMY 7:12-13 NIV

O Lord . . . save me because of your unfailing love.

PSALM 6:4 NIV

WHERE DID THAT COME FROM?

L oving the unlovable is quite a challenge. You've been there before—perhaps at work, when that smarmy coworker lied his way out of being fired and right into the cubicle next to yours. Now you get to hear his underhanded business tactics in first person. Or maybe you faced the challenge at the grocery store, when that unkempt, smelly woman with three loud rug rats bullied her way in front of you at the checkout line.

It's easy to love people who treat you respectfully. It's easy to love people who are patient, kind, and polite. It's easy to love people who smile. But those others—the mean ones, the misguided ones, the hopeless ones— now that's a different story.

On your own power, loving the unlovable comes out looking a lot like pity. Thankfully, God has a great reserve of pure love, and you can tap into it anytime you have a need.

> YOUR HEART HAS MORE SPACE FOR LOVE
> WHEN IT'S FILLED BY GOD.

A word aptly spoken is like apples of gold in settings of silver.

PROVERBS 25:11 NIV

A man finds joy in giving an apt reply—and how good is a timely word.

PROVERBS 15:23 NIV

Reckless words pierce like a sword, but the tongue of the wise brings healing.

PROVERBS 12:18 NIV

LOOKING FOR WORDS

Sarah felt like running—but that didn't seem like a very adult thing to do. Besides, what was so horrible about confronting Rhonda? Well . . . besides, er, everything. "I need to talk to you," Sarah had said on the phone, hoping her tone was friendly, not ominous. Rhonda had agreed.

"Get some help—" too confrontational. "I really care about you. Rhonda, but you're messing up big time—" still too harsh. "I can't be your friend if you keep—" ugh! There was no pretty way to say it. *Dear God, I have no clue how to talk to her*, Sarah prayed. *Please give me the right words to say.*

Just then Rhonda bounced into the room with a smile Sarah knew would soon be gone. The tears flowed, but so did the words—the right words.

Do you need to speak truthful words to rescue a friend? God is anxious to help you.

WISDOM IS SEEING LIFE FROM GOD'S PERSPECTIVE.

I keep asking that the God of our Lord Jesus Christ . . . may give you the Spirit of wisdom and revelation, so that you may know him better.

EPHESIANS 1:17 NIV

Surely you desire truth in the inner parts, you teach me wisdom in the inmost place.

PSALM 51:6 NIV

For the Lord gives wisdom, and from his mouth come knowledge and understanding.

PROVERBS 2:6 NIV

OFF THE BEATEN TRACK

Two job offers in one week—most people would be thrilled, but Randall was just confused. Should he choose to be the youth pastor at his church, or a graphic designer for a sports magazine? The choice seemed clear cut to almost everyone, except Randall. "Think of all those kids you'd be influencing," his father said with pride. "As a youth pastor, you'd be doing God's work."

Although Randall enjoyed kids, and his athletic abilities seemed to draw them to him, he felt his real talent leaned toward design, not discipleship. He asked God for wisdom to know which direction he should take, and finally he felt at peace about following his heart. The first day on the job, Randall met Simon.

"Hey, a group of us run a basketball clinic for teens on the lower east side. You interested?" he asked. Randall responded with a quick yes. He knew he'd made the right decision.

God's wisdom is available to all who ask—including you.

ALL SERVICE RANKS THE SAME WITH GOD.

With you there is forgiveness; therefore you are feared.

PSALM 130:4 NIV

For if you forgive men when they sin against you, your heavenly Father will also forgive you.

MATTHEW 6:14 NIV

Forgive whatever grievances you may have against one another. Forgive as the Lord forgave you.

COLOSSIANS 3:13 NIV

THE MIRACLE WORKER

Sally thought she was a forgiving person—until a drunk driver caused the death of her only son. Now a malignant bitterness was eating away at her. When she thought about Joe, remembered his smiling face, or looked at his picture, the only emotion she felt was hatred for the man who had carelessly taken him from her.

Sally put on her game face for family and friends. But those who knew her best, saw through her facade. "You must feel it would be impossible to forgive the man who took Joe from you," Sally's friend Cynthia said, "And you're probably right. But you can turn it over to God and place your trust in His justice. It's the only way your heart will be free to rest and heal."

Has someone inflicted an unbearable wound on your heart? Is it so big that you'll never be able to forgive it on your own? Give it to God—He's a miracle worker.

> IT IS CHEAPER TO PARDON THAN TO RESENT.
> FORGIVENESS SAVES THE EXPENSE OF ANGER,
> THE COST OF HATRED.

We are more than conquerors through Him who loved us.

ROMANS 8:37 NKJV

But thanks be to God! He gives us the victory through our Lord Jesus Christ.

1 CORINTHIANS 15:57 NIV

When you pass through the waters I will be with you; and through the rivers they will not overflow you. When you walk through the fire you will not be scorched; nor will the flame burn you.

ISAIAH 43:2 TLB

INNER BATTLES

It sounded so simple. To lose weight, you need to eat less and exercise more. But Terry had struggled with his weight all of his life. Even in grammar school, his mom bought his pants from the "husky" section. And the teasing certainly didn't help. Blame it on metabolism, poor eating habits, lousy genes, or just lack of self-control, all Terry knew was that he'd tried every new diet that came his way—without success.

So, Terry gave up dieting. Instead of counting fat grams and calories, began to pray before he ate. He simply asked for God's wisdom and self-control. Soon he found himself turning down seconds and often choosing a piece of fruit over a bag of chips. His weigh loss wasn't dramatic, but it was consistent. Terry found that a few God moments was the one thing that finally worked.

No matter what challenge you are facing, God is ready to help.

THE TOUGHEST BATTLES WE FIGHT IN LIFE ARE OFTEN WITH OURSELVES.

A sweet friendship refreshes the soul.

PROVERBS 27:9 MSG

A friend loves at all times.

PROVERBS 17:17 NIV

A man of many companions may come to ruin, but there is a friend who sticks closer than a brother.

PROVERBS 18:24 NIV

HANDS OF LOVE

Nan finished setting the table and sat down. Immediately, she thought of Jeff. Mostly, she thought of his hands. They were strong hands, to be certain. He'd helped her move three times—carried her heavy dresser up three flights of stairs for the most recent change of address.

They were gentle hands too. Hands that surrounded Nan with a hug after her mother died. Hands that prepared and brought her a meal when she was recovering from surgery. And they were capable hands. Hands that fixed a broken pipe in the middle of the night and played beautiful music on the piano.

A knock on the door woke Nan from her daydream. She walked over and peeked through the peephole. She laughed aloud at the distorted image of Jeff's hands covering his face. Nan smiled. *Those are the hands of a true friend*, she thought.

Take time today to thank God for the true friends He's placed in your life.

TRUE FRIENDSHIP IS ONE OF GOD'S MOST PRECIOUS GIFTS.

Make yourselves at home in my love.

JOHN 15:9 MSG

But I trust in your unfailing love.

PSALM 13:5 NIV

Show the wonder of your great love keep me as the apple of your eye.

PSALM 17:7-8 NIV

CUSHIONED

Try this little experiment. Get your favorite drink—a cup of coffee, hot chocolate, or maybe a glass of cold milk. Now, choose a favorite snack. Maybe it's time to open that box of cookies you've been eyeing. Ready? Okay, now find the most comfortable place in your house. Or perhaps your favorite place isn't in your house at all. Go there now.

Are you comfortable? Breathe deeply. Sip your drink. Nibble on your snack. Close your eyes if you like. Daydream about wonderful things—bike rides along a cool stream; fragrant, warm breezes after a summer rain; snowflakes drifting past the window.

Are you feeling warm? Safe? At home? That's how God wants you to feel in His love. Though the world swirls around you and often drags you into its maelstrom, God's love is always near. Soak it in. Drench yourself in it. Learn it's familiar and comforting rhythms . . . and visit often.

GOD'S LOVE IS A PLACE YOU CAN ALWAYS CALL HOME.

The heavens declare the glory of God; the skies proclaim the work of his hands.

PSALM 19:1 NIV

I praise you because I am fearfully and wonderfully made.

PSALM 139:14 NIV

For everything God created is good, and nothing is to be rejected.

1 TIMOTHY 4:4 NIV

DON'T MISS THE MIRACLES

When Robert looked back on his childhood, one of his favorite memories was of his dad's impromptu celebrations. He'd wake the kids in the middle of the night, bundle them up in old sleeping bags, then take everyone out to the backyard to watch a meteor shower. He'd interrupt dinner for a sunset or turn off the TV mid-program to redirect everyone's attention to the lightning flashing over the mountains. He'd halt a family hike to watch a line of ants carry leaves three times their size across the path. But, no matter what natural wonder happened to be taking place, his dad always said the same thing— "Thank you, God!"

Pausing to appreciate a work of art in a museum is a natural response to creativity and beauty. So is taking time to appreciate the incredible world God has made. His handiwork is everywhere. Today, why not take a walk or a drive in search of often-overlooked miracles?

THE GALLERY OF GOD'S WONDERS IS ALWAYS OPEN AND NEVER CHARGES ADMISSION.

Be kind and compassionate to one another, forgiving each other, just as in Christ God forgave you.

EPHESIANS 4:32 NIV

Bear with each other and forgive whatever grievances you may have against one another. Forgive as the Lord forgave you.

COLOSSIANS 3:13 NIV

Jesus said . . . "If you forgive anyone his sins, they are forgiven; if you do not forgive them, they are not forgiven."

JOHN 20:21, 23 NIV

TRANSFORMING GRACE

"Come on, come on, come on . . . change!" Morgan muttered at the stoplight, but to no avail. The longer he sat in traffic, the more he saw red—not just in the obstinate light overhead. He was edgy about being late for work, but more than that, he was irritated by yet another argument with his wife.

"Change, now!" he yelled at the unyielding light. He was startled by the anger he was feeling, especially when he realized that he really wanted to yell those words at his wife. That's when the thought suddenly occurred to him: I wonder how many times God's wanted to yell those same words at me?

When times get tough in relationships, it's easier to extend love to others when you recall how far God went to extend His love to you. Forgive and be forgiven—it's the highest expression of love.

FORGIVENESS IS A FUNNY THING—IT WARMS
THE HEART AND COOLS THE STING.

Steady my steps with your Word of promise.

PSALM 119:133 MSG

For he himself is our peace.

EPHESIANS 2:14 NIV

You will keep in perfect peace him whose mind is steadfast, because he trusts in you.

ISAIAH 26:3 NIV

TIGHTROPE DAY

"**I** will be unavailable for the next hour," said Marcy as she walked by three stunned faces into her bedroom. She had just endured a terrible day. It began when a truck nearly ran her off the road. Then the lunch meeting bombed. The trip to the grocery store ended in disaster as the bag with all the breakable items slipped out of her arms and onto the pavement.

If the kids had been perfect angels, she might have been able to unwind, but she had heard the arguing even before she walked into the house. And Dan probably asked about dinner politely, but she hadn't heard it that way.

Marcy opened her Bible and began to read. She knew if she stepped back into the real world too soon, she wouldn't be very loving or patient. But a quiet time with God's Word always brought back her balance.

Do you need a few God moments to still your frazzled nerves?

> **THE BIBLE REDIRECTS MY WILL, CLEANSES MY EMOTIONS, ENLIGHTENS MY MIND, AND QUICKENS MY TOTAL BEING.**

The Lord is good, a refuge in times of trouble. He cares for those who trust in him.

NAHUM 1:7 NIV

Some trust in chariots and some in horses, but we trust in the name of the Lord our God.

PSALM 20:7 NIV

I will wait for the Lord . . . I will put my trust in him.

ISAIAH 8:17 NIV

NEXT GAS, FIVE MILES

Hattie knew she was in trouble. The gauge had read "Full" for far too long to be accurate. Driving along an unknown stretch of highway on an empty tank was just asking for trouble. Just then, the engine sputtered. A few moments later, her now-silent car sat on the side of the road just a few feet from a sign that read, "Next Gas, Five Miles."

Hattie prayed for strength. Then she began walking and thanking God it was still light outside. As she continued along the empty road, she began to imagine all the terrible things that could happen to her. But then a few minutes later, she felt peace. "God is with me," she said with a smile only the birds and the lizards could see.

Bad things happen to good people. Hattie knew that. But God's promise to always be near trumped that fear.

Trust God, and the long walks won't seem so long — or so lonely.

FEAR KNOCKED AT THE DOOR. FAITH ANSWERED. NO ONE WAS THERE.

My chosen ones will have satisfaction in their work.

ISAIAH 65:23 MSG

Always give yourself fully to the work of the Lord, because you know that your labor in the Lord is not in vain.

1 CORINTHIANS 15:58 NIV

Whatever you do, work at it with all your heart, as working for the Lord, not for men.

COLOSSIANS 3:23 NIV

IS YOUR CAREER IN GEAR?

The proper wrench turns a bolt with ease. When cutting grass, a lawn mower is preferable to pinking shears. Fins work better than heels when snorkeling. Fishermen prefer poles over slingshots if they're serious about catching their limit. Obvious, right?

Then doesn't it make sense that you'll function most effectively if you work in areas that maximize the way God's designed you? It's like using the right tool for the job.

Do you really know what you're best at? It may not be what your parents always pushed you to be, or what pays the highest salary. But doing it will allow you to be the person God created you to be. So, ask your friends what they see as your strengths. Take an interest assessment test. Speak to a guidance counselor. And talk to God.

Ignoring what makes you unique can make life as uncomfortable as wearing the wrong size shoes.

HOWEVER FAR YOU GO, IT IS NOT MUCH USE IF IT IS NOT IN THE RIGHT DIRECTION.

Your righteousness is like the mighty mountains, your justice like the great deep.

PSALM 36:6 NIV

The Lord is known by his justice.

PSALM 9:16 NIV

For the Lord is God of justice. Blessed are all who wait for him.

ISAIAH 30:18 NIV

JUST DESSERTS

Children have a strong sense of justice. Perhaps it's a trait learned in the heat of battle—when your brother gets two scoops of ice cream to your one. Or maybe it's a faint echo of the character of God.

When we grow older, our sense of justice doesn't go away—it just becomes more difficult to embrace. Should you speak up about the co-worker who lied? Can you make a difference in another part of the world where people are tortured? You probably feel many things when you see injustice—anger, sadness, and perhaps helplessness.

Sometimes you can right a wrong, but often, the wrong remains unpunished. Because He is righteous, God is the perfect Judge. But here's the hard truth: God doesn't always choose to right the wrongs we see according to our timetable. There will come a time when God will speak justice into all unjust situations. But until then, you'll have to trust that He knows what He's doing.

GOD'S MILL GRINDS SLOW BUT SURE.

You are the light of the world. A city on a hill cannot be hidden. Neither do people light a lamp and put it under a bowl. Instead they put it on its stand, and it gives light to everyone in the house.

MATTHEW 5:14-15 NIV

You shine like stars in the universe as you hold out the word of life.

PHILIPPIANS 2:15-16 NIV

Let your light shine before men, that they may see your good deeds and praise your Father in heaven.

MATTHEW 5:16 NIV

BEACONS

J on and Brenda knew their neighbors well enough to expect more than a few complaints. Although most of them had decorated their houses with lights, none had a life-size manger scene filling the front yard. At least the characters were nicely crafted — they reasoned — not some plastic injection-molded monstrosities.

Jon had spent hours getting the lighting just right. It was Brenda's idea to put up the sign encouraging visitors to contact them if they wanted to know more about the "real meaning of Christmas."

As word got out, lots of cars began to drive by to see the display. Then, a week before Christmas, next-door neighbors Quentin and Marla Jackson came to the door, and Jon wondered if the display had been such a good idea after all. Maybe they're upset about the traffic, he thought.

"Jon . . . Brenda," began Quentin, "We were wondering — about your sign. You know — the real meaning of Christmas?" Are you bold enough to invite questions about your faith?

BE TO THE WORLD A SIGN THAT, WHILE WE AS CHRISTIANS DO NOT HAVE ALL THE ANSWERS, WE DO KNOW AND CARE ABOUT THE QUESTIONS.

Therefore, as God's chosen people, holy and dearly loved, clothe yourselves with compassion.

COLOSSIANS 3:12 NIV

If there is any encouragement in Christ, any incentive of love, any participation in the Spirit, any affection and sympathy, complete my job by being in the same mind, having the same love, being in full accord and of one mind.

PHILIPPIANS 2:1-2 RSV

Finally, all of you, live in harmony with one another; be sympathetic, love as brothers, be compassionate and humble.

1 PETER 3:8 NIV

JUST A PRAYER AWAY

Brenda sat down with her cup of coffee to read the paper, just as she did every morning before the chaos began. But one glance at the front page gripped Brenda's heart. The photographer had captured the despair of a young girl crying over the bodies of her parents, victims of a flood in Bangladesh.

The girl's heartache was on display for all to see, but the photo caption didn't even include her name. To most people, she would be just another nameless face in a distant country, but Brenda knew that God knew this little girl's name and cared about her pain. She bowed her head and asked Him to send someone to comfort this devastated little girl, and all the others affected by the flood.

The radio, newspaper, and television can offer a window to a hurting world. As you read today's paper, ask God to give you a heart of compassion and a commitment to prayer.

TALKING MEN FOR GOD IS A GREAT THING, BUT TALKING TO GOD FOR MEN IS GREATER STILL.

Love extravagantly.

1 CORINTHIANS 13:12 MSG

Love your neighbor as yourself.

MATTHEW 19:19 NIV

---

*Love your enemies, do good to them,
and lend to them without expecting
to get anything back.*

LUKE 6:35 NIV

OVER THE TOP

DeAnne could have used her bonus check to buy a new computer. She could have taken a much-needed vacation too, The brochures for the resort on St. Thomas sure were enticing; but DeAnne didn't spend her bonus check on herself.

Early Saturday morning, she packed her car with groceries, a microwave, clothes, and dozens of other items, and she drove across town to her sister's house. When Darlene answered the door, she was still in her pajamas. "DeAnne—what's this?" DeAnne hugged her sister and proceeded to unload the car. Darlene stood in the doorway, speechless, for at least three loads, before she came to her senses and offered to help.

"Oh, my gracious! Where did you get all of this? Why are you . . .?"

DeAnne just smiled and finished unloading the car. "It's simple, really," she finally said. "I have more than I need. And I love you."

LOVE IS NOT GETTING, BUT GIVING.

Forget the former things; do not dwell on the past. See, I am doing a new thing!

ISAIAH 43:18-19 NIV

Forgetting what is behind and straining toward what is ahead, I press on toward the goal to win the prize for which God has called me.

PHILIPPIANS 3:13-14 NIV

Jesus replied, "No one who puts his hand to the plow and looks back is fit for service in the kingdom of God."

LUKE 9:62 NIV

TAKING OUT THE TRASH

The closet was empty, but Nancy's living room had taken on the appearance of a war zone. Boxes, papers, photographs, old music records, and odds and ends littered the floor. The memory shrapnel was overwhelming.

Then Nancy picked up a photo of her college beau, Dean, and something unexpected tugged at her heart. She recalled the good times first, but soon was flooded with memories of his arrogance, the wild parties, and more than a closet full of her own mistakes.

An all-too-familiar emptiness began to seep into her heart—until she spied the blue box. It was the box she had filled with notes of encouragement after she walked away from Dean. It was the box that had built her friendship with God. Suddenly, her floor wasn't filled with precious memories—just a bunch of trash, and one very special blue box.

Have you been clinging to the past? Throw it away, and with God's help, move forward.

THE PAST IS VALUABLE AS A GUIDEPOST, BUT DANGEROUS IF USED AS A HITCHING POST.

Be still, and know that I am God.

PSALM 46:10 NIV

The Lord is my shepherd . . . he leads me beside quiet waters, he restores my soul.

PSALM 23:1-2 NIV

The Lord your God is with you, he is mighty to save. He will take great delight in you, he will quiet you with his love, he will rejoice over you with singing.

ZEPHANIAH 3:17 NIV

SHHHHH . . .

A lake with a surface like glass can only be found in just the right circumstances—no ducks searching for food, no fish bobbing to the surface, no kid skimming rocks, no underwater currents, and not a hint of a breeze. Creating a still spot in your own life may seem just as unpredictable. Hectic schedules, ringing phones, playing kids, and the constant inner dialogue of your own mind can make stillness seem impossible.

But being still is a skill to be learned. It's more than sitting down to read the Bible or chatting with God. It's actively listening while patiently waiting. It's quieting your prayer requests while longing for God's presence. It's when you hear God whisper, and come away knowing there's so much more to life than what you see with your eyes.

Whether it's ten minutes or a weekend retreat, God has something He wants to share with you. Is it quiet enough for you to hear Him?

STILLNESS IS AN ESSENTIAL PART OF GROWING DEEPER.

I want you woven into a tapestry of love, in touch with everything there is to know of God.

COLOSSIANS 2:2 MSG

Taste and see that the Lord is good.

PSALM 34:8 NIV

Praise be to the Lord, for he showed his wonderful love to me.

PSALM 31:21 NIV

GO AHEAD - TRY IT

Somewhere between milk and broccoli, children learn to be wary of trying new foods. As infants, they take whatever you give them (though sometimes much of what you give them is rapidly returned). Try suggesting a new food to a seven-year-old, however, and you're likely to hear, "But I don't like it!" even before the child has had a bite.

What about you? Do you avoid calamari? Cream corn? Cauliflower? Calves' liver? Have you ever tried a food you previously avoided, only to find out you loved it?

That's what it's like when you "taste" God's love for the first time. Though you may have avoided Him for years, when you finally discover what a relationship with God is like, you'll wish you'd met Him earlier. You may not love calamari once you've tried it, but when you discover God's love, you'll want it every day. It's a good thing He has plenty to go around.

> O LOVE OF GOD, HOW DEEP AND GREAT,
> FAR DEEPER THAN MAN'S DEEPEST HATE.

We know that in all things God works for the good of those who love him, who have been called according to his purpose.

ROMANS 8:28 NIV

Being confident of this, that he who began a good work in you will carry it on to completion until the day of Jesus Christ.

PHILIPPIANS 1:6 NIV

The Lord will fulfill his purpose for me.

PSALM 138:8 NIV

THE PAIN OF REGRET

Greg opened his eyes and looked around the room. Where was he? What had happened? It was almost two days before he could accept the news that he had fallen asleep at the wheel and caused a near-fatal head-on collision. "I'm not a terrible person," he reasoned. "It was just a terrible accident."

Still, Greg knew that his poor judgement had caused great pain and suffering for another person—a realization that left his heart aching with guilt and remorse. Sometimes the knowledge of what he had done hurt even more than his battered body.

"Feeling guilty won't change anything," a friend told him. "You must receive God's forgiveness and forgive yourself. God promises to bring something positive from even the most tragic circumstances. He will help you if you let Him."

Are you struggling with a crushing load of guilt and regret? Turn to God for help. Recovery may be slow, but His promises are sure.

IF GOD FORGIVES US, WE MUST FORGIVE OURSELVES.

I'd sell off the whole world to get you back, trade the creation just for you.

ISAIAH 43:4 MSG

Since you are precious and honored in my sight, and because I love you, I will give men in exchange for you.

ISAIAH 43:4 NIV

God has poured out his love into our hearts by the Holy Spirit.

ROMANS 5:5 NIV

LOVE STORY

It had all the makings of a great action film—some guy, sacrificing his own life to save his true love. Kara loved stories like that, but they always left her feeling inexplicably sad and empty. If only there were someone who would rescue me, she usually thought.

But this time, the story she was hearing wasn't fiction. It was coming from a church pulpit. When Kara joined her friend Carl for his church's Easter service, she had expected to hear what a horrible person she was—that she had let God down and had better get her life together. Instead, she heard that Someone came to earth to rescue her. She heard that there really was a Hero who loved her. Kara knew she'd finally found what her heart had always longed for.

Do you long for a love that is true and lasting? God has already given His life for you, and He is waiting to claim you for His own.

IT IS NOT JOUR HOLD ON CHRIST THAT SAVES YOU, BUT HIS HOLD ON YOU!

If I rise on the wings of the dawn, if I settle on the far side of the sea, even there your hand will guide me, your right hand will hold me fast.

PSALM 139:9-10 NIV

"Am I only a God nearby," declares the Lord, "and not a God far away? . . . Do I not fill heaven and earth?"

JEREMIAH 23:23 NIV

Where can I go from your Spirit? Where can I flee from your presence? If I go up to the heavens, you are there; if I make my bed in the depths, you are there.

PSALM 139:7-8 NIV

EVERYWHERE

Sharon might have discovered this truth while crossing the desert under the relentless sun. She could have uncovered it while swimming with sharks off the coast of Jamaica. Certainly she should have learned it while skydiving from 20,000 feet. How ironic, then, that she didn't experience God's promise to always be near until she was in her own backyard.

Granted, she was pinned under a pile of heavy, unrepentant firewood. Yes, she was concerned about frostbite. But somehow, she knew God was near.

Carefully, slowly, she tried again to move the pile of wood. No luck. But what she didn't notice was that a log had rolled off the back of the pile and was heading toward her Jeep—the Jeep with the built-in, too loud alarm that always seemed to go off for no apparent reason. Well . . . no apparent reason until now. Neighbors would soon arrive to investigate the noise.

Aren't you glad that God is everywhere?

WHEN THE NEED IS HIGHEST, GOD IS NIGHEST.

He who refreshes others will himself be refreshed.

PROVERBS 11:25 NIV

A generous man will himself be blessed, for he shares his food with the poor.

PROVERBS 22:9 NIV

Give, and it will be given to you. A good measure, pressed down, shaken together and running over, will be poured into your lap. For with the measure you use, it will be measured to you.

LUKE 6:38 NIV

REACHING OUT

After Jean's husband died, life never really felt like it was back to "normal." Time lessened the pain, but there was a weariness that filled her heart. She just couldn't seem to shake it.

One Saturday afternoon, Jean agreed to help a friend at a riding stable. The stable was known for its therapeutic riding program for kids with physical and emotional problems. All Jean did was help kids get on and off horses all day. She shared both laughter and frustration with the kids, but most of all, she shared their sense of accomplishment and hope. When she arrived home, Jean realized something had changed in her heart, and she knew just Who to thank for it.

God created us to live in communities. Reaching outside of your own pain to help others in the midst of theirs may be just what God uses to refresh your weary soul. How can you be a source of refreshment for someone else?

GRIEF CAN BE YOUR SERVANT, HELPING YOU TO FEEL MORE COMPASSION FOR OTHERS WHO HURT.

Even to your old age and gray hairs I am he, I am he who will sustain you.

ISAIAH 46:4 NIV

As for me, I watch in hope for the Lord, I wait for God my Savior; my God will hear me.

MICAH 7:7 NIV

Fear not, for I am with you; Be not dismayed, for I am your God. I will strengthen you, Yes, I will help you, I will uphold you with my righteous right hand.

ISAIAH 41:10 NIV

GOOD EARS

J ason's world was crumbling around him. His wife, Jill, had gone to her mother's for a few weeks. "I need some time away from our marriage," she had told him. Her absence made their best friends' announcement of their impending divorce all the more difficult to bear.

Other friends hadn't been much help, either. A few politely asked where Jill was, but they didn't seem to want to know any more than that.

This time, Jason was on his own. Well, not completely. Sitting down at the kitchen table, he began to pour out his heart to God, and God began to pour out His heart to Jason. The words weren't easy to hear, but Jason knew they were filled with truth. "Will you teach me to be a better husband?" he asked. Instinctively, he knew the answer. He just hoped God would speak to Jill too.

Have you placed your marriage in God's hands?

PRAYER IS PUTTING ONESELF UNDER GOD'S INFLUENCE.

Ask where the good way is, and walk in it, and you will find rest for your souls.

JEREMIAH 6:16 NIV

For the Lord gives wisdom, and from his mouth come knowledge and understanding.

PROVERBS 2:6 NIV

A man's steps are directed by the Lord.

PROVERBS 20:24 NIV

ROAD TO NOWHERE

Blaine was no longer just edgy. He was well over the edge. He knew the turnoff was around here somewhere, but the pouring rain was either obstructing the street sign or had washed it away all together. As he drove by the same convenience store for the third time, it crossed his mind that he should go in and ask for directions. His girlfriend would if she were here, but she wasn't. Blaine turned the windshield wipers up another notch and kept driving down the same road, not any closer to his destination than he had been an hour ago.

The idea that real men don't ask for directions is a stereotype that has been passed down in our society. In reality, regardless of gender, asking God for direction is something we should do every day—sometimes every moment. And remember, directions are useless unless we follow them.

Do you need direction for your life? Don't hesitate! God is willing and able to point you in the way you should go.

THERE'S NO BETTER COMPASS FOR LIFE THAN GOD AND HIS WORD.

There is a proper time and procedure for every matter.

ECCLESIASTES 8:6 NIV

Do not be anxious about anything, but in everything, by prayer and petition, with thanksgiving, present your requests to God.

PHILIPPIANS 4:6 NIV

Wait for the Lord; be strong and take heart and wait for the Lord.

PSALM 27:14 NIV

I DON'T GET IT

No matter how hard he tried, Stephen couldn't convince Jon to seek a relationship with God. "Why on earth would you give control of your life to some unseen being you can't really be sure exists?" he continued to ask.

As their relationship developed, Stephen grew frustrated. So he backed off and just spent time with Jon, doing life together. In prayer, Stephen still wrestled with God. "What am I doing wrong?" he would ask. His answer came a week later when he and Jon walked out of a restaurant together.

"Stephen," Jon began. "I used to think you were a real flake. But the more I know you, the more I am intrigued by your relationship with God. I think I'm ready to get to know Him a little better." Stephen suddenly realized what he had been missing: God's timing.

Are you waiting for God to answer your prayer? His answer will come at just the right time.

> IT IS FOR US TO MAKE THE EFFORT. THE RESULT IS ALWAYS IN GOD'S HANDS.

I will lie down and sleep in peace, for you alone, O Lord, make me dwell in safety.

PSALM 4:8 NIV

I carried you on eagles' wings and brought you to myself.

EXODUS 19:4 NIV

My soul finds rest in God alone; my salvation comes from him.

PSALM 62:1 NIV

CAN'T GET THERE ALONE

When was the last time you were too tired to move? After a day at the office filled with demands piled upon demands? When you finally finished moving that firewood from the driveway to the back yard? When you clicked off the kids' bedroom lights and settled into your easy chair after a day as child chauffeur and homework helper?

It's not unusual to feel too exhausted by life to seek an audience with God. That's when the prayers sound something like this: "Lord, I'll get to that quiet time right after this nap—zzzz."

There's nothing wrong with rest. Even Jesus went away to rest when He had a tough day. But, you also need time with God. Ask the God who first brought you to Him to bring you to Him once again. You'll find just enough energy to leap into His arms.

FIRST GOD BRINGS YOU TO HIM, THEN HE
BRINGS HIMSELF TO YOU.

I the Lord do not change.

MALACHI 3:6 NIV

---

*Jesus Christ is the same yesterday
and today and forever.*

HEBREWS 13:8 NIV

---

*They will perish, but you remain; they
will all wear out like a garment . . .
But you remain the same, and your
years will never end.*

PSALM 102:26-27 NIV

ROCK SOLID

Nothing is constant, except change—or so the saying goes. All it takes is a class reunion to assure you it must be true. Mr. "Most Likely to Succeed" now runs a used car lot. The quiet girl with the thick glasses is a top fashion model. The head cheerleader has five kids. The brain in biology class teaches Tae Bo. Hairlines have receded; waistlines have expanded; and expectations have been dashed, rebuilt, and redirected everywhere you look.

But it's really those who haven't changed who are up for the most ridicule. That's because change can be a positive thing, a sign of growth. But for a perfect, eternal God, it's unnecessary. He isn't fickle or moody. He won't change the rules or go back on any of His promises. And He won't love you any less when your hair turns gray or disappears altogether. Take a few moments to tell God why you're glad He never changes.

ALL BUT GOD ARE CHANGING DAY BY DAY.

The Lord detests the sacrifice of the wicked, but the prayer of the of the upright pleases him.

PROVERBS 15:8 NIV

When you pray, go into your room, close the door and pray to your Father, who is unseen.

MATTHEW 6:6 NIV

Pray in the Spirit on all occasions with all kinds of prayers and requests. With this in mind, be alert and always keep on praying for all the saints.

EPHESIANS 6:18 NIV

SHARING THE LOAD

Maureen was on her way to a meeting when the phone rang. "I know you're busy," said her friend Cindy, "but John and I are going to marriage counseling today at noon. Would you pray for us?" Maureen took out her pen and wrote Cindy's appointment in her daily calendar. Now, Maureen had an appointment, as well—an appointment with God.

Saying "I'll pray for you" is a commitment. When others ask for prayer, they're willing to share something that feels too big for them to carry on their own. Don't treat that vulnerability and responsibility lightly. When you say you will pray, mean it.

And don't give yourself a chance to forget. Write it down. Keep a prayer list. And don't forget to ask the people you pray for to let you know what God has done. Seeing God in action is a great reminder that prayer is an active, not a passive, response to those in need.

I NEED TO STOP TALKING ABOUT PRAYER—
AND PRAY.

Follow God's example in everything you do just as a much loved child imitates his father.

EPHESIANS 5:1 TLB

You are to be perfect, even as your Father in heaven is perfect.

MATTHEW 5:48 TLB

Be merciful, just as your Father is merciful.

LUKE 6:36 NIV

FOLLOW THE LEADER

Some say that dogs resemble their masters. (Or is it, people resemble their dogs?) The longer couples are married, the more they begin to look alike. If you hang around with the wrong crowd, you'll eventually end up being one of them. In other words, you grow to resemble those you spend the most time with.

Just look at a high school campus. Some teens imitate others intentionally, whether it's with hairstyles, slang, or piercing yet another body part. But after a while, unintentional imitation begins to take place as well—speech patterns, body language, and attitude. That's why parents want their kids hanging out with the "right crowd."

It's also one more reason why "hanging out" with God should be the top priority in your life. Whom better to look to for an example? Whose habits would you rather adopt, intentionally or otherwise? Take a look at your life. In what ways are you growing to resemble your Heavenly Father?

> NO MAN DOTH WELL BUT GOD HATH PART IN HIM.

Trust in the Lord with all your heart and lean not on your own understanding.

PROVERBS 3:5 NIV

Those who know your name will trust in you, for you, Lord, have never forsaken those who seek you.

PSALM 9:10 NIV

I will trust and not be afraid. The Lord, the Lord, is my strength and my song.

ISAIAH 12:2 NIV

TRUST AND OBEY

Lee could have sworn that Josie was smiling. If dogs could smile, that is. She'd won a blue ribbon in the obedience class for the third year in a row. As Lee gave her a warm hug and a treat, a thought crossed his mind. I bet I could tell Josie to run right onto a busy freeway, and she'd do it without hesitation.

What a responsibility! Josie trusted him so much that the Aussie would do whatever he said, the moment he said it. She'd even do things that, from a dog's point of view, might seem rather foolhardy. What would it take for me to trust God's love for me as much as Josie trusts mine for her? he wondered.

In God's eyes, you're not a pet or even a servant. You're a beloved child. When He leads you in a direction you hesitate to go, what's keeping you from trusting in His love?

IT IS NOT OUR TRUST THAT KEEPS US, BUT THE GOD IN WHO WE TRUST WHO KEEPS US.

Teach me what I cannot see.

JOB 34:32 NIV

But as for me, O Lord, deal with me as . . . one who bears your name.

PSALM 109:21 TLB

Show me the path where I should go, O Lord; point out the right road for me to walk.

PSALM 25:4 TLB

PARENTAL PERSPECTIVE

"**N**o, Joey! Put it down!" Colleen yelled at her two- year-old son from across the kitchen. Surprised by the tone of his mother's voice, Joey immediately dropped the knife on the floor and began to cry. Colleen tenderly picked up the tow-headed toddler and held him tightly in her arms. She must have left the knife on the table after cutting his apple for lunch. "A knife is not a toy!" she tried to explain, feeling a mixture of guilt and relief.

He's just too little to understand, she thought. I guess sometimes "because I said so" is the only answer I can really give. Colleen suddenly thought of God as her Parent and realized, I guess that's also the only answer God can give sometimes too.

Just like toddlers reaching for a shiny knife, God's children often ignorantly reach for, or pray for, things that could harm them. We need to remember that God's answers are always motivated by love.

> OUR GOD DOES NOT ALWAYS ANSWER OUR PRAYERS AS WE REQUEST. BUT HE DOES FOR US, AS FOR OUR LORD IN THE GARDEN; HE STRENGTHENS US.

*Take a good look at God's wonders—
they'll take your breath away.*

PSALM 66:5 MSG

Stop and consider God's wonders.

JOB 37:14 NIV

*I will praise you, O Lord, with all my
heart I will tell of all your wonders.*

PSALM 9:1 NIV

GREAT EXPECTATIONS

The drizzle gave way to low-lying fog. The headlights on Julie's car could barely cut through the heavy blanket of gray mist. She'd never driven home for the holidays, always preferring to take a plane. But this year, her tight budget made her settle on a road trip instead. The route was unfamiliar, and for the last four hours, the scenery was indiscernible.

For a brief instant, the thick clouds in front of her parted, revealing a snow-capped mountain peak. Its sheer, vertical face filled her windshield from top to bottom. She was awestruck. The glimpse of grandeur disappeared as quickly as it had come. But now that she knew it was there, the drive seemed different, filled with hidden wonder.

There are no ordinary days. Glimpses of God and His handiwork are everywhere, surprising you when you least expect it. Nurturing an appreciation for holy wonder can make every day an adventure.

WHAT GOD DOES, HE DOES WELL.

From the fullness of his grace we have all received one blessing after another.

JOHN 1:16 NIV

Let them give thanks to the Lord for his unfailing love and his wonderful deeds for men, for he satisfies the thirsty and fills the hungry with good things.

PSALM 107:8-9 NIV

Praise the Lord, O my soul, and forget not all his benefits.

PSALM 103: 2 NIV

AMAZING GRACE

"Bless us, O Lord, for these Thy gifts which we are about to receive." As a little girl, Grace had always loved that prayer. She'd secretly believed it was named after her, or she after it. She was never quite sure which. But as an adult, Grace felt that praying before meals was nothing more than a well-intentioned tradition—until Jeff and his family came to dinner.

As they sat down at the table, Jeff asked her if he could say the blessing. "Of course," she said politely and bowed her head. But his words took her by surprise. He sounded truly grateful, speaking from the heart. From that day on, Grace—both the woman and the prayer before meals—was never the same.

When you thank God for His blessings in your life, is it more like a thank-you card your parents have forced you to write, or a love letter from your heart?

PRAYER REQUIRES MORE OF THE HEART THAN THE TONGUE.

Delight yourself in the Lord and he will give you the desires of your heart.

PSALM 37:4 NIV

I delight greatly in the Lord; my soul rejoices in my God. For he has clothed me with garments of salvation.

ISAIAH 61:10 NIV

Then will I go to the altar of God, to God, my joy and my delight.

PSALM 43:4 NIV

CHANGE OF HEART

"Delight" and "desire" were two of Gary's favorite words. He desired a new car and was delighted when it was finally his. He desired success because he found delight in the admiration of others. He desired happiness, so he was delighted to live in America, where its pursuit was his inalienable right.

When he learned that God said He'd give him the desires of his heart, Gary was delighted to make God's acquaintance. But things didn't turn out quite the way Gary had planned. Over time, he discovered that God was a source of delight that never grew old. Gradually, the desires of his heart began to change, and then he realized God was doing exactly what He'd promised.

What are the deepest desires of your heart? What has God done to fill them? What do you delight in most often? Is anything standing in the way of you delighting in God?

> A MAN'S HEART IS RIGHT WHEN HE WILLS
> WHAT GOD WILLS.

Faith is being sure of what we hope for and certain of what we do not see.

HEBREWS 11:1 NIV

It is by faith you stand firm.

2 CORINTHIANS 1:24 NIV

Since we have been justified through faith, we have peace with God.

ROMANS 5:1 NIV

FATHER KNOWS BEST

You don't need to be an optometrist to know that God's eyes are not the same as yours. They witnessed the creation of the world. They watched you being formed in your mother's womb. They can look straight into your heart.

That's where faith comes in. To begin to see things through God's eyes, you first have to grow to trust His heart. Like any relationship, trust builds over time. But it's put to the test when you believe God loves you, yet circumstances seem to be screaming the exact opposite. That's when you need to remember you don't have the ability to see every situation through God-colored glasses. You can only see the present and the past, while God can look ahead to the future.

Is there any circumstance in your life that makes you doubt God really has your best interest in mind? What is the best reassurance that He does?

ALL I HAVE SEEN TEACHES ME TO TRUST THE CREATOR FOR ALL I HAVE NOT SEEN.

The Lord is near to all who call on him.

PSALM 145:18 NIV

The Lord is far from the wicked but he hears the prayer of the righteous.

PROVERBS 15:29 NIV

I tell you, whatever you ask for in prayer, believe that you have received it, and it will be yours.

MARK 11:24 NIV

FREE AND CLEAR

Russ resisted the idea of a cell phone for years. Contrary to many of his friends, he actually wanted to have times in his life when no one could find him. But this afternoon, he was thankful his wife had given him a phone for Christmas, because his tire was as flat as the Texas prairie. Unfortunately, his spare seemed to have had sympathy pains, so here he sat.

Russ tried to make a call, but nothing happened. He'd have been happy to pay roaming charges, but apparently there wasn't anywhere close enough to roam to. So much for my emergency back-up plan, he thought. I guess God's the only One who can hear me now.

Prayer is like a cell phone with God's number on speed dial. God never counts minutes, applies roaming charges, or limits your prime time access. Best of all, recharging your relationship doesn't even take an adapter. It happens the moment you say, "Lord—"

WHEN THE OUTLOOK IS BAD, TRY THE "UPLOOK".

Be strong in the Lord and in his mighty power.

EPHESIANS 6:10 NIV

Strengthen me according to your word.

PSALM 119:28 NIV

The name of the Lord is a strong tower; the righteous run to it and are safe.

PROVERBS 18:10 NIV

KEEPING FIT

Kaye opened the door to the gym with a sense of purpose. For months now, she'd been meeting with Brad at 6 A.M. As her personal trainer, he'd helped Kaye lower her heart rate, improve her stamina, and drop a dress size. But last week's conversation by the rowing machine had gotten her thinking.

In this conversation, she had casually mentioned to Brad that her busy schedule didn't allow her much time to spend with God one-on-one. "Hey," he replied, "If you've got time to work out, you've got time to work in!"

Exercising only your abdominal muscles doesn't constitute a balanced workout. In the same way, keeping your body in shape while ignoring your soul will result in a flabby spiritual life. God created you with a body, mind, and spirit. All of them need regular exercise to help you stay healthy inside and out, and God is the perfect personal trainer. Have you scheduled a regular appointment with Him?

> THERE IS NO BETTER WAY TO FINISH THE SPIRITUAL LIFE THAN TO BE EVER BEGINNING.

In this world you will have trouble. But take heart! I have overcome the world.

JOHN 16:33 NIV

Dear friends, do not be surprised at the painful trial you are suffering, as though something strange were happening to you.

1 PETER 4:12 NIV

For a little while you may have had to suffer grief in all kinds of trails. These have come so that your faith . . . may be proved genuine.

1 PETER 1:6-7 NIV

WHIRLWIND

There was little left, besides a pile of torn linens and clothing. The tornado had touched down, destroying one home and leaving another untouched just a block away. The newspaper referred to it as an "act of God," but Terry couldn't reconcile that in her mind. How could the loving God she knew be any part of this senseless devastation?

She sat down on the pile of rubble where her home used to be. This happens to other people on the front pages of distant newspapers, not to my family and me, she thought. Then, the question "Why not?" popped into her mind. She knew life held both blessing and heartache, and for the first time, she could truly empathize with those who'd felt the latter. She also realized she could pray to the one who would be there through it all.

In this world, the unexpected happens. There'll be both good times and bad. Does your relationship with God differ during those times?

WHEN EVERYTHING FALLS APART, IT'S TIME
TO LET GOD BUILD SOMETHING NEW.

Revive us, and we will call on your name.

PSALM 80:18 NIV

Lord, when doubts fill my mind, when my heart is in turmoil, quiet me and give me renewed hope and cheer.

PSALM 94:19 TLB

I keep right on praying to you, Lord. For now is the time—you are bending down to hear. You are ready with a plentiful supply of love and kindness.

PSALM 69:13 TLB

HOLY GROUND

The only way to face a Monday morning, especially a rainy one, was with a cappuccino grande. Or should she go for the mocha latte? As usual, Lana was undecided when it was her turn at the counter to order. There were so many choices. The only thing she always ruled out was anything decaffeinated. "What a waste of coffee beans, " she'd say.

Lana was the first to admit she was probably addicted to caffeine, but she sure liked the way nursing a tall, warm mug made her feel. As she finished up, she felt comforted and ready to face the day. Kind of like a quiet time in a cup! she chuckled to herself.

Spending time with God is caffeine for your soul, without any addictive side effects. It's always ready when you are, no special equipment or brewing time required. Best of all, the cup never runs dry.

SPENDING TIME WITH GOD IS FILLED WITH PERKS.

Once more I will astound these people with wonder upon wonder.

ISAIAH 29:14 NIV

For by him all things were created: things in heaven and on earth, visible and invisible, whether thrones or powers or rulers or authorities; all things were created by him and for him.

COLOSSIANS 1:16 NIV

For everything God created is good, and nothing is to be rejected if it is received with thanksgiving.

1 TIMOTHY 4:4 NIV

FLIGHT OF FANCY

Troy taxied the private plane into the small county airport. It had been another perfect flight: great weather, beautiful scenery, and the joy of soaring above the hustle and bustle of life. Although he'd had his pilot's license for almost six months now, he never ceased to be amazed at the intricacy of a plane's instrumentation and design. I can't imagine having a brain that could come up with something like this, he thought.

At that exact moment, an ordinary gray-and-white pigeon flew past the cockpit window. Troy hardly would have noticed it on any other day, but today he looked at it through the eyes of a pilot. The bird had no instrumentation, yet it possessed such ease, beauty, and agility in flight. Man's greatest creations can't hold a candle to God's simplest wonders, he marveled. He took a moment to thank God for the beauty of His creation.

Have you thanked God for the beauty around you today?

GOD IS AN ARTIST, AND CREATION, HIS GALLERY.

The plans of the Lord stand firm forever, the purposes of his heart through all generations.

PSALM 33:11 NIV

God is not a man that he should lie, nor a son of man, that he should change his mind.

NUMBERS 29:13 NIV

The Lord will carry out his purpose.

JEREMIAH 51:12 NIV

DIVINE DESIGN

The movie was about to start. Jill hurried to the women's restroom, not wanting to miss a moment of the three-hour epic ahead of her. After washing her hands, she hurriedly reached above her head for a towel. Instantly, water from her wet hands rolled merrily down her wrists and into the sleeves of her baggy sweater.

"Who were these things designed for, the LA Lakers?" she muttered. "You'd think someone designing a restroom would have figured out the benefits of reaching down for a towel, instead of up!"

As she made her way back to her seat, Jill laughed at herself and shared a brief moment with God. *It's a good thing that You put more thought into Your plans than people do! You didn't make the world on a whim, did You?*

No. God's plans unfold always at a perfect pace with an understanding of your past, present, and future. You can be certain of that.

THE BLUEPRINTS OF LIFE WERE DRAWN BY A
HEART OF LOVE.

Weeping may remain for a night, but rejoicing comes in the morning.

PSALM 30:5 NIV

Let us not become weary in doing good, for at the proper time we will reap a harvest if we do not give up.

GALATIANS 6:9 NIV

Those who sow tears will reap with songs of joy. He who goes out weeping, carrying seed to sow, will return with songs of joy carrying sheaves with him.

PSALM 126: 5-6 NIV

HOPE FOR HEALING

When Phil got out of bed, he realized something was missing. He bent over and twisted to the right. The pain wasn't there anymore. After his back surgery, he had debated which was worse — the ailment or the cure. But today, he found himself whistling as he hurried down to breakfast, thanking God for a day without excruciating pain.

That pain had made even the brightest day feel like the dead of night. There were times when he thought he couldn't stand it anymore — when it hurt to stand up and it hurt to lie down. Some nights seemed as if they would last forever. The only relief he found was in those moments of prayer when he felt God's assurance that someday the pain would end. When it didn't happen overnight, he almost lost hope. But finally, that morning came, and the pain was gone for good.

If you are in pain today, God can see you through it.

GOD DRIES TEARS FROM THE INSIDE OUT.

May he give you the desire of your heart and make all your plans succeed.

PSALM 20:4 NIV

You (Lord) have granted him the desire of his heart and have not withheld the request of his lips.

PSALM 21:2 NIV

Delight yourself in the Lord and he will give you the desires of your heart.

PSALM 37:4 NIV

PERFECT GIFTS

"Cosmic Kill-joy" — that's what Ginny called God. Believing God existed was one thing; putting her life in His hands was quite another. "God wants prune-faced missionaries, not professional cellists," she'd convinced herself.

After months of struggling to pay the bills without abandoning her music, Ginny finally gave up. More out of desperation than love or commitment, she prayed, "Okay, God, You win. If You want me to give up the cello and get a 'real job,' I'll do it. You know I'm afraid to say this, but please, lead me where You want me to go." To her surprise, God didn't lead her to some faraway country. Instead, when she took her nephew to his piano lessons, she stepped into a God moment — a children's program was looking for someone to teach the cello.

When you surrender your dreams to God, you will be squarely on the road to fulfilling them.

THE ONLY GIFT GOD GIVES THAT EVER NEEDS TO BE RETURNED IS HIS LOVE.

He makes me lie down in green pastures, he leads me beside quiet waters, he restores my soul.

PSALM 23:2-3 NIV

I will lie down and sleep in peace, for you alone O Lord, make me dwell in safety.

PSALM 4:8 NIV

For he (God) grants sleep to those he loves.

PSALM 127:2 NIV

LIGHTS OUT

It was well past one o'clock in the morning, but Kaye could, tell her daughter's slumber party was winding up, not down. She tried to think back to when she was that age, but she couldn't remember the appeal of delirious exhaustion.

As she made her way down the stairs one more time to ask the girls to quiet down, she found herself thanking God for dreaming up sleep. "If You didn't stop us, we'd never stop ourselves," she philosophized with a yawn.

She stood at the doorway and watched her sleepy-eyed daughter yawn as she listened to her best friend. "Steph," Kaye said, "The human body was designed to shut down at the end of the day. Take a hint, and turn out the lights!" All the girls grumbled, but she thought she saw gratefulness in her daughter's eyes.

When was the last time you thanked God for the blessing of restful sleep?

CONSERVE ENERGY . . . GO TO BED ON TIME.

Set your minds on things above, not on earthly things.

COLOSSIANS 3:2 NIV

Our citizenship is in heaven. And we eagerly await a Savior from there.

PHILIPPIANS 3:20 NIV

Do not store up for yourselves treasures on earth . . . But store up for yourselves treasures in heaven where moth and rust do not destroy.

MATTHEW 6:19-20 NIV

LIVING FOR THE LONG RUN

Working with the youth group energized Corey—most of the time. But the dark clouds that were on the horizon this morning were now directly overhead. All he wanted to do was stay home and watch the football game on TV, but he knew the threat of a downpour would make the scavenger hunt all the more exciting in the kids' eyes.

When he arrived, the rain had already started to fall. A teen from the group ran up to him with an umbrella. "I'm so glad you came, Mr. Johnson," Clay said. "Remember that talk we had last week about prayer? Could I ask you a couple of questions?" Corey couldn't help but smile. He knew the time he spent today was much more important than any football score.

Corey wasn't motivated by a desire to receive recognition for his efforts; he was interested in making an eternal difference in the lives of others. What motivates you?

WHY NOT INVEST YOUR LIFE IN SOMETHING THAT GIVES ETERNAL RETURNS?

All the days ordained for me were written in your book before one of them came to be.

PSALM 139:16 NIV

O Lord, you have searched me and you know me.

PSALM 139:1 NIV

He will take great delight in you.

ZEPHANIAH 3:17 NIV

RARE BREED

A rare Siberian tiger paced anxiously behind the bars. Any tiger was bound to be rare in Milwaukee, but one with blue eyes and a white- and black-striped coat stood apart from the rest. Cherie explained to her young son about endangered species. She told him that when something was extinct, nothing like it would ever be born on the earth again.

"Kinda like me," Chad replied. "God made only one me, so I guess that means I'm an endangered species too." Cherie started to contradict her son, but something in his deep blue eyes made her stop. In a way, he was right. There'd never be another Chad. A picture of her son wearing an "Endangered Species" sign around his neck popped into her head. I wonder if the world would treat him any differently? she thought.

In God's eyes, you are one of a kind. No wonder He thinks you are so special.

WHEN GOD MADE YOU, HE DID BREAK THE MOLD!

Whoever would draw near to God must believe that he exists and that he rewards those who seek him.

HEBREWS 11:6 RSV

I will give them a heart to know me, that I am the Lord.

JEREMIAH 24:7 NIV

You who seek God, may your hearts live!

PSALM 69:32 NIV

THE BIG PICTURE

Sundays were fairly predictable around the Johnson household. Sunday school was at 9:00 and worship at 10:30. Church was followed by a trip to the all-you-can-eat buffet by noon and an afternoon nap. Joe and Mary Lou Johnson then spent an hour with the Sunday paper and watched an occasional sporting or social event. Nothing exceptional ever happened.

Sunday had become just like every other day for them. Even being in the presence of God seemed mundane. "Do you ever feel like we re just going through the motions at church?" Mary Lou asked.

"All the time," Joe replied, laying the newspaper in his lap.

Instead of ignoring the issue, they started to talk—really communicate—about how to regain the mystery and intimacy of their relationship with God. Humbled by His greatness, the couple held hands and asked Him to renew their faith.

How is your relationship with God? Is it time for you to renew your faith?

> KNOWING GOD IS COMPREHENDING HE'S TOO
> BIG TO BE TRULY KNOWN.

All you have made will praise you, O Lord.

PSALM 145:10 NIV

For you created my inmost being; you knit me together in my mother's womb. I praise you because I am fearfully and wonderfully made.

PSALM 139:13-14 NIV

Worship the Lord with gladness; come before him with joyful songs . . . It is he who made us.

PSALM 100:2-3 NIV

A MOUNTAIN, A HAWK, AND PRAISE

The last hundred yards made up for the previous half-mile of shifting rocks and shirt-snagging underbrush. It was almost as if the mountain had admitted defeat and offered up an easy path to Cindy and Brian. They wove their way to a large, flat boulder and climbed onto it.

"Wow! Look at that!" Brian exclaimed.

The treetops below swayed gently in the breeze. A hawk soared gracefully overhead. Tiny mountain flowers smiled in the sunshine. The rhythm of this natural world was unfamiliar to two college kids weaned on computers and television.

Cindy spun slowly to soak up as much as possible. "It's as if all or nature is singing out to the Creator," she said in awe.

Time passed much too quickly, and as they climbed down the rocky path, they were silent. They didn't want to interrupt the most excellent praise and worship service they'd ever experienced.

> IF YOU WANT TO KNOW WHAT PRAISE LOOKS LIKE, STUDY A BIRD IN FLIGHT, A FLOWER IN BLOOM, OR THE PURPLE-HUED SILHOUETTE OF A MOUNTAIN RANGE.

My God turns my darkness into light.

PSALM 18:28 NIV

---

*Your word is a lamp to my feet and a
light for my path.*

PSALM 119:105 NIV

Let us walk in the light of the Lord.

ISAIAH 2:5 NIV

WINNING STRATEGY

"Pin the tail on the donkey" isn't just a children's party game. It's a lesson in theology. All you need is a blindfold, a few disorienting twirls from a friend, and you're on your way to who-knows-where. With a thumbtack in hand and a prayer you don't trip over anything in your path, the only things guiding you are your gut instinct and the disheartening laughter of your peers as you head the wrong way. Sound a lot like life?

Thankfully, God doesn't leave you blindfolded as you stumble through life. He's given you a map in the form of the Bible. Just like every map, it has a key that will help you understand how to read it. God's key is prayer. It's the combination of reading His Word and listening for what He wants to say to you through it that will guide you. Are you missing either the map or the key in your times with God?

LIFE IS A ROAD MAP THAT GOD UNFOLDS A DAY AT A TIME.

I have kept the ways of the Lord; I have not turned from my God to follow evil.

PSALM 18:21 NLT

The man of integrity walks securely.

PROVERBS 10:9 NIV

May integrity and uprightness protect me, because my hope is in you.

PSALM 25:21 NIV

EVERYWHERE

Considering how long it took to get his promotion, it was quite a shock for Mike's friends when they heard he'd quit his job. In disbelief they said, "You're kidding, right?" "What are you doing?" and "I can't believe it!"

What his friends didn't know was how good it felt to leave a company that prided itself on deception. All his friends could see was the glory and prestige of a vice-president title—and the huge paycheck. But Mike saw how the almighty dollar had turned good people into power-hungry rule-benders. No matter how good the money was, he knew it was time to move on.

Living a life of integrity can mean big sacrifices at times. But those are the times when you have to do the right thing and trust God with the consequences. If you are facing such a dilemma today, don't compromise. Let God show you His formula for success. It's always a winning proposition.

OUR HEAVENLY FATHER NEVER TAKES ANY THING FROM HIS CHILDREN UNLESS HE MEANS TO GIVE THEM SOMETHING BETTER.

He is faithful in all he does.

PSALM 33:4 NIV

The Lord your God is God; he is the faithful God, keeping his covenant of love to a thousand generations of those who love him and keep his commands.

DEUTERONOMY 7:9 NIV

To the faithful you show yourself faithful.

2 SAMUEL 22:26 NIV

ETERNALLY STEADFAST

Have you ever broken a promise? Told a lie? Turned your back on a friend? Betrayed a confidence? Ignored someone in need? Ever? You may consider yourself a faithful friend, employee, spouse, or parent, but can you say that you're faithful in "all" you do? That's a tall order. In fact, it's an impossible order unless you're God.

Though your own unfaithfulness should give you pause, it can also be an object lesson in what God is not. Even with the best of intentions, you will fail. Eventually, you will prove yourself unfaithful in something you say or do or even think. But God cannot be unfaithful.

What does that mean to you? What kind of relationship does that mean you can have with God? Do you have a hard time believing that's true? If so, why? Take a few moments to list ways God has shown Himself faithful in your life.

FAITH IS USELESS, UNLESS THE ONE IT IS PLACED IN IS FAITHFUL.

---

*Become friends with God; He's already
a friend with you.*

2 CORINTHIANS 5:20 MSG

---

*There is a friend who sticks close than
a brother.*

PROVERBS 18:24 NIV

---

*Anyone who chooses to be a friend of
the world becomes an enemy of God.*

JAMES 4:4 NIV

LAST, BEST FRIEND

Many of Pete's peers thought he was a nerd, and some of them didn't even know he existed. For the first sixteen years of his life, he spent a lot of time feeling sorry for himself because he had no friends. Just when he would think he'd found someone he could talk to, his family would move. "I'm sorry, son. That's the life of a military family," his father would say.

Then, when he moved his junior year in high school, everything changed. First, he found a friend in Nick. Ironically, Nick moved away just a few weeks later, but not before he introduced Pete to his youth group. One Sunday night, during a youth group worship service, Pete found a permanent friend: God. From that day on, he knew he would always have someone to talk to. He had found a friend who wouldn't move.

Are you looking for a friend who will always be there for you? Turn to God, and you will find a forever friend.

A FRIEND IS A PRESENT YOU GIVE YOURSELF.

Though your riches increase, do not set your heart on them.

PSALM 62:10 NIV

If I have put my trust in gold . . . if I have rejoiced over my great wealth . . . then these also would be sins to be judged.

JOB 31:24-25,28 NIV

The love of money is a root of all kinds of evil.

1 TIMOTHY 6:10 NIV

DIVINE DIVIDENDS

E very August, Sylvia got a bonus. It was company policy across the board. Although the amount varied from year to year, it was always enough to buy something on her lengthy wish list—a new electronic gadget, a piece of furniture, a full-body treatment at a spa.

Yes, every August, Sylvia had the check in her hands. But unfortunately, by May or June, she already had a credit card statement reflecting some purchase for the bonus she'd not yet received. Worse yet, this year her company decided to discontinue their bonus benefit, but not before she'd already charged the purchase of a new laptop computer.

Faced with the bill and the realization she'd be paying on it for quite a long time, Sylvia gathered the courage to face something else. She'd chosen to depend on money rather than God, to fill her life with joy.

Do you have joy in your life? Are you trusting God for it, or something far less reliable.

THE ONLY DEBT WORTH OWING IS GRATITUDE.

I will bless the Lord and not forget the glorious things he does for me.

PSALM 103:2 TLB

Since we are receiving a kingdom that can not be shaken, let us be thankful, and so worship God.

HEBREWS 12:28 NIV

Give thanks in all circumstances, for this is the will of God for you.

1 THESSALONIANS 5:18 NIV

SINCERELY YOURS

Card racks at stationery stores are loaded with ways to say thanks. There are cards that pop out, fold up, or even record a personal message. They can make you laugh or bring a tear to your eye. You can even write your own sentiments in a blank card. Gratitude is big business. But is it big enough?

Even if you sent thank-you cards to everyone in your life who ever deserved one, which would be a fairly overwhelming job in itself, what would you send to God? Would you find the most expensive card, add a bouquet of flowers—which, of course, He actually gave you first- and send them to Him every day of your life? Every hour? Every minute? How could you possibly thank Him enough?

There's only one thank-you card worthy of a Father such as yours—the living, breathing card of your life, lived in a way that reflects His love.

> A GRATEFUL HEART WRITES A THANK-YOU
> NOTE TO GOD WITH EVERY BREATH.

I call as my heart grows faint; lead me to the rock that is higher than I.

PSALM 61:2 NIV

The Lord is my strength and my song; he has become my salvation.

EXODUS 15:2 NIV

It is God who arms me with strength and makes my way perfect.

2 SAMUEL 22:33 NIV

ENDURING THE UNENDURABLE

There are plenty of reasons to give up in life: fear, exhaustion, discouragement, complacency, pain, anger, impatience, and embarrassment, to name just a few. There are also those obstacles that just refuse to budge.

What have you given up on in life? It may be a project, a dream, or a relationship. It may even be hope or faith. What was your breaking point?

There will always be mountains that will rise beyond your endurance. There will be times when turning back seems like a wise thing to do. But the next time you're ready to give up, first ask yourself a couple of questions: Is this something I just don't want to face, or can't face, on my own? Am I giving up because I'm trying to accomplish this in my own strength instead of turning to God? Then, pray and ask God to help you climb the mountain you are facing.

IT TAKES MORE COURAGE TO FINISH A BATTLE THAN TO BEGIN IT.

The Lord your God is with you. . . . He will take great delight in you, he will quiet you with his love, he will rejoice over you with singing.

ZEPHANIAH 3:17 NIV

Look at the birds, free and unfettered, not tied down to a job description, careless in the care of God. And you count far more to Him than the birds.

MATTHEW 6:26 MSG

When you pass through the waters, I will be with you; and when you pass through the rivers, they will not sweep over you. When you walk through the fire, you will not be burned.

ISAIAH 43:2 NIV

LETTERS OF LOVE

L ove letters come in all forms. Some are scribbled on napkins and placed in children's lunchboxes. Some are covered with X's and O's. Others are composed with such heartfelt emotion that they're read over and over, until the paper has worn thin and the words are barely discernible. They touch the heart and warm the soul.

The Bible is God's love letter to the world. But even more importantly, it's a personal message to you. The words may remain the same for everyone, but God's relationship with you is different than His relationship with anyone else. How He communicates through those words, and what they will mean in relation to your life, will also differ. Cherish God's love letter to you, and read it over and over until you know the words by heart. It's more than a textbook or book of stories, and like a love letter, it's to be treasured.

WHEN YOU READ GOD'S WORD, YOU MUST CONSTANTLY BE SAYING TO YOURSELF, "IT IS TALKING TO ME, AND ABOUT ME."

Blessed are the pure in heart, for they will see God.

MATTHEW 5:8 NIV

Like a weaned child with its mother, like a weaned child is my soul within me.

PSALM 131:2 NIV

Whoever humbles himself like this child is the greatest in the kingdom of God.

MATTHEW 18:4 NIV

OUT OF THE MOUTHS OF BABES

You've probably heard something like this while in line at the grocery store: "Mom, why is that woman so fat?" "Mommy, isn't this the checkout lady you don't like?" "Look at that man with the funny face!" There's a time in every child's life when unfiltered truth spills out freely, often creating rather embarrassing situations.

But in addition to the embarrassing moments, there are precious ones. "Mom, God is painting pictures with the clouds!" "God's love is kinda like my pillow—all soft, and it smells like home." "I know we can't hear bunnies talk, but I bet God can."

Jesus asks you to become like a little child so you can see God clearly. The more you fill up your life with routine and a daily wheel-barrow full of trouble, the cloudier your vision will become. But when you become like a child, you will find that birds sing "Awesome God;" watercolors drip off God's paintbrush, forming rainbows; and God goes bowling in the thunder.

YOU CAN SEE GOD BEST WHEN YOU LOOK THROUGH A CHILD'S EYES.

Even when walking through the dark valley of death, I will not be afraid; for you are close beside me guarding, guiding all the way.

PSALM 23:4 TLB

Defend your people, Lord; defend and bless your chosen ones. Lead them like a shepherd, and carry them forever in your arms.

PSALM 28:9 TLB

Though he give you the bread of adversity . . . yet he will be with you to teach you—with your own eyes you will see your Teacher.

ISAIAH 30:20 TLB

A TIME TO UPROOT

"I don't want to go." Six-year-old Jessie dropped to the bare floor, crossed her legs, and folded her arms. The last of the boxes had been loaded on the moving truck.

Karen sat down next to her daughter. "Honey, we can't stay here. Another family is moving in. Remember, you met their little boy?"

Jessie started to cry. "I don't want him to have my room."

"You know we have to move, Jessie. Daddy has a new job in Texas. Don't you think we should go with him?" Jessie's chin quivered. Karen hugged the little girl with her father' blue eyes. "Sometimes we just have to do hard things."

Jessie sighed and asked, "Is this one of those times?"

"Yes, honey," her mother replied.

You may not understand why God has allowed certain circumstances in your life. But you can know that He is right there in the midst of them with you. Together, you can do anything, no matter how difficult it might seem.

FAITH MAKES ALL THINGS POSSIBLE . . .
LOVE MAKES ALL THINGS EASY.

For what is a man profited, if he shall gain the whole world, and lose his own soul?

MATTHEW 16:26 KJV

Whoever loves money never has money enough; whoever loves wealth is never satisfied with his income.

ECCLESIASTES 5:10 NIV

You cannot serve both God and Money.

LUKE 16:13 NIV

ONE OF EACH

"The one who dies with the most toys wins" had been Tim's motto since he graduated from college. But he never felt satisfied with what he had and was always shopping for more. Days before each paycheck, he would wander the aisles at the local electronics superstore making a mental list. It never mattered that he probably already had a recent model at home.

Did he need all that stuff? Nope. The fact is, he made quite a good living as an architect. He owned a beautiful home, drove a nice car, and enjoyed fancy dinners out six times a week. But each week he'd always end up at that store.

Finally, Tim realized he was trying to fill up the emptiness inside with more and more material things, and he knew it couldn't be done. He decided to find out if God's love could fill his empty heart.

Are you trying to fill your heart with things? Maybe it's time to let God in.

A MANS'S TREATMENT OF MONEY IS THE MOST DECISIVE TEST OF HIS CHARACTER, HOW HE MAKES IT AND HOW HE SPENDS IT.

Seek, and ye shall find; knock, and it shall be opened unto you.

MATTHEW 7:7 KJV

If from there you seek the Lord your God, you will find him if you look for him with all your heart and with all your soul.

DEUTERONOMY 4:29 NIV

I love those who love me, and those who seek me find me.

PROVERBS 8:17 NIV

SEARCH PARAMETERS

Stephanie had spent most of the day looking for things. Before work, she looked for her car keys, which she finally found under the kitchen table. At the office she looked for the Jones' file and found it had slipped behind the cabinet and was being guarded by a fierce-looking spider.

After work, she searched the refrigerator, freezer, and every kitchen cabinet three times, looking for something to eat. She finally chose a frozen pizza, which she couldn't bake until she'd located the missing cookie sheet. When she couldn't find the pizza cutter, she gave up and used a clean pair of scissors instead.

As she ate her pizza, Stephanie wondered what else she would have a difficult time finding before the day was over. Whispering a prayer, she thanked God that He couldn't be misplaced. She'd found Him dozens of times during the day— mostly to ask for patience.

God is always as close as your whispered prayer.

IF YOU CAN'T FIND GOD USING A TELESCOPE, TRY AN OUTSTRETCHED HAND.

Be strong and courageous. Do not be terrified; do not be discouraged, for the Lord your God will be with you wherever you go.

JOSHUA 1:9 NIV

Whatever I have, wherever I am, I can make it through anything in the One who makes me who I am.

PHILIPPIANS 4:13 MSG

It is better to take refuge in the Lord than to trust in man.

PSALM 118:8 NIV

NOT TOO HEAVY

Belinda was disillusioned soon after she'd become a Christian. "Your life will never be the same," her friends had told her. But her problems remained.

"So what's supposed to be different?" she asked Darcy one day.

"Well, we still have problems. One difference is that we have Someone to share them with," her friend said.

Belinda's frustration turned to curiosity. "You mean God?"

"Yes," Darcy answered.

"Is He going to pay my rent too?"

Carefully and thoughtfully, Darcy explained God's promise to always be near and His promise of rest for weary souls. Then she added, "You've been flying solo for a long time, Belinda. Just hang in there with God, and let Him sit in the pilot's seat for a change."

When God comes into our lives, our problems don't just disappear. But we do receive a new perspective. God can lead you to solutions. But mostly, the problems just seem more manageable with the Creator of the universe by your side.

The greater the difficulty, the more glory in surmounting.

SKILLFUL PILOTS GAIN THEIR REPUTATION FROM STORMS AND TEMPESTS.

Even though on the outside it often looks like things are falling apart on us, on the inside, where God is making new life, not a day goes by without His unfolding grace.

2 CORINTHIANS 4:16 MSG

The grace of our Lord was poured out on me abundantly.

1 TIMOTHY 1:14 NIV

It is good for our hearts to be strengthened by grace.

HEBREWS 13:9 NIV

TERRIBLE, HORRIBLE, EXCELLENT DAY

The kids were particularly loud in the basement, but Judy couldn't hear them. She was outside mending the broken relationship with her neighbor. "I'm so sorry the kids hit your bird feeder with their baseball. We'll pay for it, of course, and I'll make sure they're more careful." When Bruce walked in the door from work with a bandaged right hand, Judy knew life was going to get more difficult for a while. The day had been a disaster.

But when Judy, Bruce, and their three children sat down at the dinner table, all was right with the world. Following supper, they laughed while playing table games. After stories and bedtime prayers, Bruce and Judy plopped onto the couch. "The world is falling apart . . ." she began.

He finished her thought, "But God is still in our hearts."

God has poured out His grace m our hearts—enough to get us through every trial.

GOD'S LOVE WORKS FROM THE INSIDE, OUT.

Who out there has a lust for life? Can't wait each day to come upon beauty?

PSALM 34:12 MSG

He has made everything beautiful in its time. He has also set eternity in the hearts of men.

ECCLESIASTES 3:11 NIV

The Lord reigns, he is robed in majesty . . . Your throne was established long ago; you are from all eternity.

PSALM 93:1-2 NIV

SEEING EVERYTHING NEW

Chris had forgotten a lake could be the host to so many different sounds. Wind whistled. Birds chirped and squawked. And every once in a while bubbles raced to the surface with a tiny "pop." The scenery was spectacular too. Instead of one mountain vista, he saw two—the second reflected in the glassy water. Though he loved his computer tech job, these were the moments he longed for.

Paula slipped onto the log next to Chris. "What do you see out there?" she whispered.

"It's not what I see out there; it's what I feel inside." Paula nodded in understanding. "You know I love my work," he said. "It invigorates me. But being in the middle of God's creation makes me feel so alive. It's as if He created this moment just for me—to show me what eternity feels like."

When was the last time you paused for a few moments to drink in a glimpse of eternity?

> WHEN YOU EMBRACE BEAUTY, YOU EMBRACE GOD.

At day's end I'm ready for sound sleep, for you, God, have put my life back together.

PSALM 4:8 MSG

He grants sleep to those he loves.

PSALM 127:2 NIV

You will be secure, because there is hope; you will look about you and take your rest in safety.

JOB 11:18 NIV

DEEP REST

Sleepless nights—Vic had experienced hundreds of them. As a child, he didn't sleep because of severe allergies. He'd lie awake gasping for air and grasping for his inhaler. The teen years brought new sleep challenges because he was worried about his parents' divorce and his grandfather's terminal cancer. After college, his job stress doubled, and the nights became short once again. For a time, he tried sleeping pills. When he used them, he slept, but woke up tired.

Out of desperation, Vic went looking for help. Counselors listened, but their solutions were temporary at best. It was a good friend who finally found the answer: a forced time of silence at the beginning and end of the day. Sleep began to come easier. Then Vic filled that time with prayer. Each day, he prayed for energy and peace. He got both. Now he sleeps deeply. Insomnia has been banished. But even beyond a good night's sleep, Vic has found something else: true rest.

THAT WE AREN'T MUCH SICKER AND MUCH MADDER THAN WE ARE IS DUE EXCLUSIVELY TO THAT MOST BLESSED AND BLESSING OF ALL NATURAL GRACES, SLEEP.

Nothing is secret that will not be revealed, nor anything hidden that will not be known and come to light.

LUKE 8:17 NKJV

Would not God have discovered it, since he knows the secrets of the heart?

PSALM 44:21 NIV

This will take place on the day when God will judge men's secrets.

ROMANS 2:16 NIV

UNDERCOVER OPERATION

M ark heard his wife's scream over the sound of the shower. He threw a towel around himself and hurried downstairs. What he didn't expect to find was his wife doubled over with laughter.

"Mona! You scared me to death," Mark said, annoyed. "What happened?"

Mona, with tears of laughter, pointed to the crawlspace doorway. There was the sack of potatoes Mark had tossed in a couple of months ago and had promptly forgotten. In the damp darkness, the potatoes had happily sprouted, wildly sending shoots in every direction, blocking the entire doorway.

Some things grow best in the dark. Secrets, for instance. Is there anything in your life you don't want others to know? A habit or addiction? Your credit card balance? Your past? Bringing secrets to light can be painful, but keeping them in the dark only allows them to grow. You can trust the light of God's love to help you clean out the crawl space of your heart.

NOTHING IS SO BURDENSOME AS A SECRET.

Keep company with God, get in on the best.

PSALM 37:4 MSG

As the deer pants for streams of water, so my soul pants for you, O God.

PSALM 42:1 NIV

I myself will see him with my own eyes—I, and not another. How my heart yearns within me!

JOB 19:27 NIV

THE BIG GAME SHOW

Religion was like a series of game shows to Evan. When he first began exploring, he felt like he was spinning the Wheel of Fortune. *Which beliefs will I land on today?* he wondered, and he went from one religion to another, always coming away dissatisfied.

Studying the history of religions, he joined the panel of To Tell the Truth, asking the question, "Will the real God please stand up?" And when he became discouraged yet again, he felt like a kindergarten contestant on an adult-level episode of Jeopardy, who was saying, "What is—I don't have a clue, Alex?"

Christians believe that spiritual fulfillment is about relationship: a personal relationship with a God who knows us and wants to be involved in our lives—a God who loved us so much that He made a way for us through the sacrifice of His son. This plan is recorded in the Bible, a book that promises if we earnestly seek truth, we will find it. Seek truth earnestly and hones to every mind its choice between truth and repose.

> GOD OFFERS TO EVERY MIND ITS CHOICE
> BETWEEN TRUTH AND REPOSE.

Be generous and willing to share.

1 TIMOTHY 6:18 NIV

Good will come to him who is generous and lends freely.

PSALM 112:5 NIV

A generous man will prosper; he who refreshes others will himself be refreshed.

PROVERBS 11:25 NIV

UNDESERVED ABUNDANCE

The woman in the tollbooth refused Simon's outstretched dollar bill. "The gentleman in the car ahead of you paid your toll, sir," she explained. Confused, Simon stumbled over a word of thanks and quickly drove off in search of the car that proceeded him. When he finally caught up with the white sedan, he glanced at the driver, but he did not know him.

Simon motioned to the mysterious benefactor to roll down his window. "Why'd you pay for me?" he yelled across the lane.

The man just waved, yelled a friendly, "Have a good day," and disappeared into the morning traffic. Simon was baffled. Something for nothing—God's the only one who does stuff like that, he thought. But he felt good, unexpectedly blessed. That's when he decided that on the way home, he'd surprise whoever was behind him by paying his or her toll.

Blessings are undeserved, yet God showers you with them every day. How can you pass the joy on to others?

> **BE KIND: EVERYONE YOU MEET IS FIGHTING A HARD BATTLE.**

God's there, listening for all who pray, for all who pray and mean it.

PSALM 145:18 MSG

I love the Lord because he hears my prayers and answers them. Because he bends down and listens, I will pray as long as I breathe.

PSALM 116:1-2 TLB

He has not despised my cries of deep despair; he has not turned and walked away. When I cried to him, he heard and came.

PSALM 22:24 TLB

NO DEAF EAR

The little voice coining from the hack bedroom was just loud enough to be heard over the hum of fans blowing in the basement. "Dear God, I thought you promised no more floods? Anyway, help our basement get dry real fast and help Dad not to worry about it."

"Did you hear that, Ben?" Janna asked.

The scowl and furrowed brow that had arrived with the discovery of four inches of water in the basement melted into a smile. "I guess the second half of that prayer got answered pretty quickly," he said to his wife. "And the other half will be taken care of soon. I wish I could pray like that."

Do you wish you could pray like a child—asking God for something and expecting it to happen? After a few disappointing "Where was your answer, God?" prayers, it's pretty easy to imagine God isn't listening. But children know the truth: God is listening.

FAITH IS NOT BELIEVING THAT GOD CAN, BUT THAT GOD WILL!

Life rooted in God stands firm.

PROVERBS 12:3 MSG

Blessed is the man who does not walk in the counsel of the wicked . . . He is like a tree planted by streams of water, which yields its fruit in season.

PSALM 1:1,3 NIV

But I am like an olive tree flourishing in the house of God.

PSALM 52:8 NIV

HOW DOES YOUR GARDEN GROW?

When Tom opened the drapes on the sliding glass door facing his backyard, he was confronted with a jungle. He and his family had only been gone for three weeks, but their backyard looked like it had been abandoned for months. *How'd the weeds grow that fast?* he thought. Three weeks of inattention certainly showed; not only in his yard, he realized, but also in his relationship with God.

When Tom went on vacation, he liked to forget everything. Other than an occasional prayer at the dinner table, he hadn't really given God much thought during those three weeks. But as he surveyed the overgrowth in his garden, it occurred to him that God had still been thinking a lot about him. So before Tom attacked the backyard, he first took some time to pull some spiritual weeds in his soul.

When you head off on vacation to enjoy the things that God has created, do you leave your relationship with Him behind?

> **WHEN YOU HAVE SHUT YOUR DOORS AND DARKENED YOUR ROOM, REMEMBER . . . YOU ARE NOT ALONE, BUT GOD IS WITHIN.**

Open up before God, keep nothing back; he'll do whatever needs to be done.

PSALM 37:5 MSG

Search me, O God, and know my heart, test me and know my anxious thoughts.

PSALM 139:23 NIV

The crucible for silver and the furnace for gold, but the Lord tests the heart.

PROVERBS 17:3 NIV

BREAKING RUSTED LOCKS

D ennis wedged the crowbar in between the lock and the latch on the cabinet. Snap! The latch broke off with such force that he fell backward, and stumbled into a row of bicycles that fell like dominos.

"Well, I deserved that," he said to himself. He opened the cabinet. Stacks of pornographic magazines filled the two shelves. After a brief pause, he began tossing the magazines into a big trash bin. "Okay, God," he prayed, "You know my darkest secrets. Now please help me to find the light again."

With the shelves empty, Dennis wheeled the bin to the backyard and dumped its contents onto the already burning fire. When the fire died down, he returned to the garage. He picked up the latch with the lock still attached and targeted the trashcan. But then he stopped mid-toss. Instead, he took the lock to his office and set it on his desk. It remains there as a reminder to keep nothing from God. And it's working.

WHY COMES TEMPTATION BUT FOR MAN TO
MEET AND MASTER AND MAKE CROUCH
BENEATH HIS FOOT?

It is strength that endures the unendurable and spills over into joy.

COLOSSIANS 1:11-12 MSG

It is God who arms me with strength and makes my way perfect.

2 SAMUEL 22:33 NIV

The Lord is my strength and my song; he has become my salvation.

ISAIAH 12:2 NIV

JUST ENOUGH

Warren struggled to get the dryer into his truck.

"Hang on!" Sam shouted, and he trotted over to help him lift the bulky object onto the truck bed.

On the way to the dump, they listened to the radio together until a pothole knocked the unpredictable device into its "not gonna work" mode. "You need to fix that," said Sam.

"Yeah. When I have the money," replied Warren nonchalantly.

"Tell me, Warren. Why is it you're always so positive and so unfazed by things that go wrong?" Sam asked. "If my car stereo died, I'd be selling blood to get the money to replace it. Plus, you've been through some tough stuff lately with work and your girlfriend moving away so suddenly. Doesn't any of this stuff bother you?"

Warren thought a moment, then replied, "If I counted on my own strength, I'd still be trying to lift that dryer, so to speak. But God gives me enough strength to endure all things."

THE CARE OF GOD FOR US IS A GREAT THING,
IF A MAN BELIEVE IT AT HEART: IT PLUCKS
THE BURDEN OF SORROW FROM HIM.

God, a most fierce warrior, is at my side.

JEREMIAH 20:11 MSG

The Lord will fight for you; you need only to be still.

EXODUS 14:14 NIV

Do not be afraid of them; the Lord your God himself will fight for you.

DEUTERONOMY 3:22 NIV

CHARMED LIFE

D o you believe in good luck charms? Do you carry a rabbit's foot, avoid walking under ladders, read your horoscope, wish on falling stars, or cross your fingers? If a friend tries something new, do you say, "Good luck"? If so, why?

At times, knowing God may feel like you've found a good luck charm. After all, you have His protection, His love, and His guidance. But God isn't a lucky rabbit's foot to help keep bad things from happening to you. His Word isn't a fortune cookie holding pithy little sayings that you can pick and choose as blessings for your life.

God's power cannot be measured or tamed. He's not your Genie in a bottle or magic Wishing Well. He's the Ruler of the universe and Lord of all. God is a mighty Warrior, and the good news is He's fighting for you.

HEAVEN'S HELP IS BETTER THAN EARLY RISING.

Seek peace and pursue it.

PSALM 34:14 NIV

---

*Make every effort to live in peace
with all men.*

HEBREWS 12:14 NIV

---

*Let us therefore make every effort to
do what leads to peace and to
mutual edification.*

ROMANS 14:19 NIV

A PEACEFUL PURSUIT

"Peace on earth, goodwill toward men" isn't just a sentiment on a Christmas card. It was initially a greeting straight from Heaven. Having God's peace in your heart is one thing. But, what does peace on earth look like? Is it just a platitude, or do you think it can take place in your daily life? Is it something God will bring about, or are you part of the solution?

Peace is often pictured as a quiet, pastoral scene, almost devoid of movement. But peace can he found in the laughter of friends as easily as in solitude and meditation.

Sometimes making peace takes work; it has to be pursued. If there is a conflict in a relationship, you may have to confront a person in love in order to find peace again. Ask God for help as you strive to pursue and maintain peace in all of your relationships; and most importantly, ask Him to fill your life with His peace.

PEACE IS LIBERTY IN TRANQUILLITY.

We never really know enough until we recognize that God alone knows it all.

1 CORINTHIANS 8:3 MSG

In all things God works for the good of those who love him.

ROMANS 8:28 NIV

If you, then, though you are evil, know how to give good gifts to your children, how much more will your Father in heaven give good gifts to those who ask him.

MATTHEW 7:11 NIV

NOT AS SMART AS WE THINK WE ARE

K aren spoke first. "I think God is teaching us a lesson."

Ned snorted his disagreement and replied, "I don't think God would ruin someone's life just to teach us a lesson. We just live in a fallen world."

"Or maybe," added Sue, "Gretchen is the one being taught a lesson."

Karen wasn't so sure. "God wouldn't cause Gretchen's husband to have a car accident simply to make a point!"

The three friends sat in silence for a few minutes, sipping coffee and waiting for Gretchen. When she arrived, Karen said, "Gretchen . . . we heard the news . . . if there's anything we can do—"

Gretchen smiled weakly and said, "Well, you could thank God for Len's accident." The three sudden looks of surprise were almost enough to make Gretchen laugh. "If not for the accident, we wouldn't have known that Len had cancer. They did surgery immediately and believe they got it all. We are so grateful!"

GOD KNOWS BEST WHAT IS BEST. WHY THEN SHOULD WE QUESTION HIM?

Thanks be to God for his indescribable gift!

2 CORINTHIANS 9:15 NIV

A gift opens the way for the giver.

PROVERBS 18:16 NIV

That everyone may eat and drink, and find satisfaction in all his toil— this is the gift of God.

ECCLESIASTES 3:13 NIV

OVERFLOWING

By the end of the day the boxes had been delivered—twenty-seven in all. Phil felt tired, but satisfied. He and Samantha had created a unique gift box for each family in the study group.

For the Howards, they boxed up food and gift certificates for local department stores.

The Lawsons got a box of kitchen gadgets so they could create the gourmet meals they loved to fix with the best cookware.

Terry's box contained a record player and a gift certificate for a local music store.

Phil and Samantha even gave themselves a box—mostly to hide their identity as the gift-givers. "It's the best thing we've ever done," said Phil. "Since God has given us so much, it was obvious how we should spend that inheritance." When they opened their gift, they feigned surprise at the contents: dozens of movie ticket vouchers. "Hey, we could share these with our friends!" Phil said with a smile.

WE ARE NEVER MORE LIKE GOD THAN WHEN WE GIVE.

Satisfy us in the morning with your unfailing love, that we may sing for joy and be glad all our days.

PSALM 90:14 NIV

Let the morning bring me word of your unfailing love, for I have put my trust in you.

PSALM 143:8 NIV

In the morning, O Lord, you hear my voice; in the morning I lay my requests before you and wait in expectation.

PSALM 5:3 NIV

CLEAN START

J erry hopped out of the shower, rejuvenated. He gave his hair a quick comb and headed down to the chair in the family room. As he sat down, ready to spend a few moments with God, it dawned on him that his time here every morning was like shower number two. First, he washed the outside. Then, it was time for the inside. He couldn't imagine starting his day any other way.

How do you start your day? Taking a few moments with God not only helps wash away the mistakes of the day before, but it also gives you a boost of physical, emotional, and spiritual energy that helps set the tone for your entire day. A little TLC is all you need. Why not let Talking (prayer), Listening (taking time to hear God's reply), and Contemplation (reading a few verses of Scripture and considering how God would like you to apply them to your life) be a shower for your soul?

I CAN TELL YOU THAT GOD IS ALIVE BECAUSE I TALKED WITH HIM THIS MORNING.

All scripture is inspired by God and profitable for teaching, for reproof, for correction, and for training in righteousness.

2 TIMOTHY 3:16 RSV

I have hidden your word in my heart that I might not sin against you.

PSALM 119:11 NIV

Your statutes are my heritage forever; they are the joy of my heart. My heart is set on keeping your decrees to the very end.

PSALM 119:111-112 NIV

SCRIPTURE SURFING

The premium cable package was finally at Greg's fingertips. He sat down with the remote control, ready for action. He could choose between sports, movies, news, weather, music videos, animals, history, or exciting travel destinations. He could improve his golf swing, pick up a foreign language, or buy his wife an anniversary gift without ever getting out of his easy chair. He was overwhelmed with all of the options.

That's how Greg felt about the Bible too. He never knew if he should start at the beginning, follow a Bible study book, or open it randomly and pick out a "verse for the day." He knew the Bible contained everything he needed to face life: information on healing relationships, tips on marriage and parenting, and lists of things to do and not to do. Yet, once again, he was overwhelmed with all of the options.

Remember, the Bible isn't a crash course in life; it's a conversation with the living God. If you're unsure where to start, seek out some guidance, and then plunge in.

BE ASTONISHED THAT GOD SHOULD HAVE WRITTEN TO US.

The righteous will live by faith.

ROMANS 1:17 NIV

Now faith is being sure of what we hope for and certain of what we do not see.

HEBREWS 11:1 NIV

Continue in your faith, established and firm, not moved from the hope held out in the gospel.

COLOSSIANS 1:23 NIV

FAITH WALK

"I won't follow a God I can't understand," was Jason's standard reply to anyone who tried to talk to him about spiritual things. "Why is there suffering? How could God create the world out of nothing? Why would Someone that powerful care about me anyway?"

Kurt knew Jason's questions were valid, but his reasoning was faulty. "Do you really understand how a heavy, metal plane flies through the air?" he asked him. Jason had to admit he didn't. "But you still fly in one," Kurt continued. "You don't understand the chemistry behind cold medicine, but you take it when you need it. You admit you don't know how life began, but that doesn't stop you from taking your next breath. That's what faith's all about."

No, we can't see or understand God, but we can see and feel signs of His love for us everywhere. And He's our Maker, our Heavenly Father—that's why He cares.

ONLY TO OUR INTELLECT IS GOD INCOMPREHENSIBLE; NOT TO OUR LOVE.

He has showed you, O man, what is good. And what does the Lord require of you? To act justly and to love mercy and to walk humbly with your God.

MICAH 6:8 NIV

Love the Lord your God, listen to his voice, and hold fast to him.

DEUTERONOMY 30:20 NIV

My sheep listen to my voice; I know them, and they follow me.

JOHN 10:27 NIV

QUESTIONS OF CONSCIENCE

The cashier handed Stephen his change. With a quick thank you, Stephen headed out the door, putting the cash in his wallet. But how could there be a ten? he wondered. He'd just paid for lunch with the only bill he had—a ten. He realized the cashier must have mistakenly thought he'd handed her a twenty. He turned to go back when something inside him asked, Why? You sure could use the extra cash.

He knew his wife would return it. She'd feel that's what God wanted her to do because it was the right thing. But Stephen wasn't so sure about all this God stuff. But, if God wasn't real, why did walking out with this money feel so wrong? Stephen walked back inside to return the money.

God has built into us an inner moral voice, our conscience. Listen to what that voice is saying to you; then act accordingly. This is the way to establish inner peace.

> GOD LOOKS AT THE CLEAN HANDS, NOT THE FULL ONES.

We know that in everything God works for good with those who love him, who are called according to his purpose.

ROMANS 8:28 RSV

"For I know the plans I have for you," declares the Lord, "Plans to prosper you and not to harm you, plans to give you hope and a future."

JEREMIAH 29:11 NIV

Many, O Lord my God, are the wonders you have done. The things you have planned for us no one can recount to you.

PSALM 40:5 NIV

THE BIG PICTURE

This was the most difficult puzzle Monty and Cindy had ever attempted. "One thousand pieces!" Monty said when he dumped the box onto the dining room table.

"We'll be eating in the kitchen for months," Cindy responded. Still, they both enjoyed a good challenge.

A few days later, they sat around the dining room table, struggling to fill in a difficult puzzle section. "Does this look black or dark green to you?" Cindy asked.

"Black—maybe. This would be a lot easier if Yukon hadn't eaten the box."

"He only ate half of the picture. We can figure out the rest—right?"

Three weeks later, they finally regained use of the dining room. They'd given up on the puzzle. It was too difficult without the picture to work from. Life is like that. But—God has a copy of the completed puzzle. When we lose sight of the picture, He still knows where the pieces fit.

EVERY MAN'S LIFE IS A PLAN OF GOD.

Pray hard and long. Pray for your brothers and sisters. Keep your eyes open.

EPHESIANS 6:18 MSG

———————————

The prayer offered in faith will make the sick person well.

JAMES 5:15 NIV

———————————

Pray for those who persecute you.

MATTHEW 5:44 NIV

PART OF THE SOLUTION

Tony did a double-take. It had to be them. Even ten years couldn't disguise the familiar faces of his former next-door neighbors. Tony recalled the last time he'd seen them. They were barely speaking to each other when they put their house on the market. Their divorce was almost final. The memory was anything but a pretty picture.

Now here they were at a marriage conference, looking far from divorced. Tony watched them looking attentively into each other's eyes as they spoke; he noted their interlocked hands. At the break, he'd go say hello. But for now, he took a moment to thank God for letting him see an answer to an almost forgotten prayer. It felt great to know he played a part in the miracle he was witnessing right now.

Your prayers are part of a greater picture, one you may never fully see. But when you catch of glimpse of what God has done, it's time for praise.

> **MORE THINGS ARE WROUGHT BY PRAYER THAN THIS WORLD DREAMS OF.**

Be doers of the word, and not hearers only, deceiving yourselves.

JAMES 1:22 RSV

Not everyone who says to me, "Lord, Lord," will enter the kingdom of heaven, but only he who does the will of my Father who is in heaven.

MATTHEW 7:21 NIV

What good is it, my brothers, if a man claims to have faith but has no deeds? . . . Faith by itself, if it is not accompanied by action, is dead.

JAMES 2:14,17 NIV

LOUD HANDS

D o you know the sound of twelve hands hammering? Lowell and his family do. One of those hands is his; another, his wife's. But the other ten? They're neighbors and strangers finishing up the framing on what will become Lowell's first home. His income made it difficult for him to get a traditional loan. But that didn't stop his friends from helping him fulfill a life-long dream.

Lowell didn't seek formal assistance programs— didn't fill out any applications. His help came from a group of caring people with some free time and a desire to make life better for Lowell's family.

In two months, Lowell and his family will enjoy their first night under the new roof. A roof, by the way, that won't be completed for another week or so, when today's twelve hands will he joined by twelve more. What a sound that will be!

When was the last time you helped to make someone else's dream come true?

WE ARE HERE TO ADD WHAT WE CAN TO LIFE, NOT TO GET WHAT WE CAN FROM IT.

Better is one day in your courts than a thousand elsewhere.

PSALM 84:10 NIV

Godliness with contentment is great gain.

1 TIMOTHY 6:6 NIV

My soul finds rest in God alone.

PSALM 62:1 NIV

GROUNDED

J ust driving on the road to the airport filled Peggy with wanderlust. She could so easily picture herself unloading her bags, then waiting in line under a sign that read "Athens," or "Paris." But that was her brother's reality, not hers. Today, she was taking Roy to the airport so he could fly to Cairo for a photo shoot. Afterward, she would return home to finish up the laundry.

As Roy got out of the car, bags in hand, Peggy was ready for her usual twinge of jealousy. But instead, she felt an ache that prompted her to pray. Roy's schedule was filled with exotic destinations, but his heart was empty. He had no interest in knowing the God who created the wonderful world he photographed.

Driving home, Peggy felt not only content, but also blessed. She knew her laundry room would hold more joy for her than the pyramids would for Roy. Praise came mixed with tears.

CONTENTMENT IS REALIZING THAT GOD HAS ALREADY GIVEN ME EVERYTHING I NEED FOR MY PRESENT HAPPINESS.

Draw near to God and he will draw near to you.

JAMES 4:8 RSV

But as for me, it is good to be near God.

PSALM 73:28 NIV

"Return to me," declares the Lord Almighty, "And I will return to you."

ZECHARIAH 1:3 NIV

PERRY'S CHAIR

The chair in the family room was Perry's. This was where he sat to watch the World Series, to read the newspaper, and to "rest his eyes" during the late-night news.

Recently, his chair had acquired a new role. His daughter had given him a Bible sectioned off with a reading for each day, so one could read it through in a year. He'd always been intimidated by the "Good Book," not knowing where to start. But, he decided he'd give it a try. Maybe he'd learn something new.

As he began to read, he came upon stories he'd never heard—and some he'd heard, but not in such detail. Every day, he'd put on his reading glasses, sink back into the chair, and read: Old Testament to New Testament. And somehow, as he read, something began to form; a sense of God and of human beings that he'd never known. And he gained a sense of just where he fit into the picture—all from the comfort of his chair.

THE BIBLE IS MEANT TO BE BREAD FOR OUR DAILY USE, NOT JUST CAKE FOR SPECIAL OCCASIONS.

We urge you, brothers, warn those who are idle, encourage the timid, help the weak, be patient with everyone.

1 THESSALONIANS 5:14 NIV

Let us not give up meeting together, as some are in the habit of doing, but let us encourage one another.

HEBREWS 10:25 NIV

Preach the Word; be prepared in season and out of season; correct, rebuke, and encourage— with great patience and careful instruction.

2 TIMOTHY 4:2 NIV

CHAIN REACTION

Maybe it was not enough hot water to finish his shower that morning. Maybe it was a restless night's sleep. Maybe it was indigestion or a cold coming on. Whatever it was, Jeremy was in a bad mood. And everyone who crossed his path would know it.

When he got up, he kicked the dog, who chased the cat, who tormented the rat, and on and on. You know the story. But picture what Jeremy passed on to the people he connected with that day — his wife and kids, his boss and coworkers, the waitress at the coffee shop, and the phone solicitor who called at dinner time. If only Jeremy had taken a moment to reconnect with God during the day and acknowledge his lack of patience and kindness for those around him, he could have broken the cycle. But, instead, Jeremy was on a roll.

Life isn't lived in a vacuum. Your actions affect everyone around you. Choose to be a positive influence in other people's lives each day.

YOU CANNOT ADD TO THE PEACE AND GOOD WILL OF THE WORLD IF YOU FAIL TO CREATE AN ATMOSPHERE OF HARMONY AND LOVE RIGHT WHERE YOU LIVE AND WORK.

The prayer of a righteous man has great power in its effects.

JAMES 5:16 RSV

Answer me when I call to you, O my righteous God. Give me relief from my distress; be merciful to me and hear my prayer.

PSALM 4:1 NIV

The Lord accepts my prayer.

PSALM 6:9 NIV

THE VIRTUE OF STRONG KNEES

Jamie knelt and began scooping up the tiny plastic building blocks. A spread of red, white, yellow, and blue pieces covered her son Scot's bedroom floor. "I love you, Scot, but you've got to learn how to pick up your room," she called out. Scot was plopped down in the hallway with a bucketful of toy cars.

Scot was a wonderful boy, but Jamie knew there was a long road ahead for her youngest son. The trail of disappointment and frustration left by her older, high-school son proved that.

Lord, she began to pray silently, *I know You love Scot. Help him to grow up strong and love you more than anything.* As she shuffled around on her knees, she suddenly realized she'd knelt on a plastic wheel. "How odd! I didn't even feel that," she said aloud.

"It's because you have strong knees, Mommy," Scot answered.

Spending time on your knees in prayer will help you deal with the struggles of life.

IF YOUR KNEES ARE SHAKING, KNEEL ON THEM.

Heal me, O Lord, and I will be healed; save me and I will be saved, for you are the one I praise.

JEREMIAH 17:14 NIV

Show me the path where I should go, O Lord; point out the right road for me to walk.

PSALM 25:4 TLB

My eyes are ever looking to the Lord for help, for he alone can rescue me.

PSALM 25:15 TLB

UNDER-QUALIFIED

Penny entered the grocery store. Her friend Sharon was on her mind. Penny had tried cheering her up with cards, flowers, phone calls, a new job, and financial assistance. But nothing seemed to help; Sharon was still floundering. *Maybe I should set her up with that nice single guy at work*, she thought.

The sound of crying interrupted her thoughts. A little girl stood bawling in front of the frozen foods. Penny tried calming her down, but the girl was inconsolable. Before Penny could contact security, the girl's frantic mother came around the corner. One moment in her mother's arms, and the girl was smiling. She just needed her mom, thought Penny.

Sharon came to mind again. Suddenly, she recognized why all her efforts to help had failed. She needs her Father, not me, she thought. Instead of continuing to plan, Penny began to pray.

Are those you are helping becoming dependent on you—or God?

WITHOUT GOD, WE CANNOT. WITHOUT US, GOD WILL NOT.

He who walks with the wise grows wise, but a companion of fools suffers harm.

PROVERBS 13:20 NIV

Blessed is the man who does not walk in the counsel of the wicked . . . but his delight is in the law of the Lord.

PSALM 1:1-2 NIV

Do not be yoked together with unbelievers.

2 CORINTHIANS 6:14 NIV

UNDER THE INFLUENCE

Has a red shirt ever ended up in your washing machine with a load of whites? What happens? Pink socks for everyone. The red shirt may not seem to fade much, but it sure leaves its mark on everything around it.

The same thing happens when you spend a lot of time with people who do things that go against God's law of love. You begin to pick up their "hue." Consider using God's name as a curse, for instance. This may not be a habit you've struggled with, but after spending time with people to whom it's second nature, you may not notice it much anymore. It may even seem humorous, at times. The next thing you know, words you never thought you'd say are slipping out of your mouth.

This doesn't mean you should never spend time with people whose values differ from God's. You can't love people without spending time with them. But if their habits begin influencing your own, watch out. You soon may find yourself in hot water.

GOOD COMPANY AND GOOD DISCOURSE ARE THE VERY SINEWS OF VIRTUE.

Everyone should be quick to listen, slow to speak and slow to become angry.

JAMES 1:1V NIV

The Lord is compassionate and gracious, slow to anger, abounding in love.

PSALM 103:8 NIV

A fool gives full vent to his anger, but a wise man keeps himself under control.

PROVERBS 29:11 NIV

SHORT FUSE

A muddy trail led upstairs, right to Brittany's room. Sonya headed up to confront her daughter. As usual, she was on the phone; her room was a disaster, including the pile of clothes Sonya had just washed that morning. Sonya grabbed the phone out of her hand before her daughter could even voice her good-byes. "I didn't do it! It's not my fault!" was Brittany's angry retort to her mother's insistence that she clean the carpet this minute.

"How stupid do you think I am?" Sonya snapped back. "You left a trail!" Sonya slammed the door on her way out. Though she was fuming, she could hear God whisper how out of control she was. In her anger, she denied any wrongdoing, accusing Brittany of being the real culprit. She heard herself saying, "It's not my fault!" but stopped short when she heard God's reply: You left a trail.

Even when we don't tell ourselves the truth, God will.

> TWO THINGS FILL THE MIND WITH EVER NEW AND INCREASING WONDER AND AWE—THE STARRY HEAVENS ABOVE ME AND THE MORAL LAW WITHIN ME.

Offer right sacrifices and trust in the Lord.

PSALM 4:5 NIV

What I want from you is your true thanks; I want your promises fulfilled. I want you to trust me in your times of trouble, so I can rescue you, and you can give me glory.

PSALM 50:14-15 TLB

Trust in the Lord and do good. Dwell in the land and cultivate faithfulness. Delight yourself in the Lord and he will give you the desires of your heart.

PSALM 37:3-4 NIV

DESERVED REWARDS

The quarter fell smoothly through the coin slot. Continuing his mid-afternoon workday tradition, Aaron pushed the button above his favorite candy bar. But something went awry. Out dropped a piece of fruit. Aaron uttered a few choice words. He'd been duped. He returned to his desk, muttering, and tossed the banana in the trash.

An hour later, he was still upset. Realizing this seemed more than a bit excessive, he asked God for some insight. What he got in return was more than he expected. Earlier that morning Aaron had asked God to help him get the promotion he'd been waiting for. It was given to another co-worker instead, and Aaron had felt duped.

Many of us, consciously or unconsciously, see God as a cosmic Vending Machine—prayers in and we'll get what we've "ordered." God does want the very best for us, but "God's best" isn't always what we see as best for us. It's through constantly seeking Him (not some magic formula) that we will find what He desires for us.

WE LITTLE KNOW THE THINGS FOR WHICH WE PRAY.

Everything is possible for him who believes.

MARK 9:23 NIV

If you believe, you will receive whatever you ask for in prayer.

MATTHEW 21:22 NIV

Ask and it will be given to you; seek and you will find; knock and the door will be opened to you. For everyone who asks receives; he who seeks finds; and to him who knocks, the door will be opened.

MATTHEW 7:7-8 NIV

CAPTURING THE IMPOSSIBLE

Six months had passed since the plant closed and Jerry lost his job as a machinist. As he sat alone at the kitchen table staring at the growing stack of unpaid bills, he felt himself sinking into an ocean of despair.

He had filled out dozens of applications and followed every lead, but he knew there was one thing he still had not done. Bowing his head, he began to pour out his heart to God. "It's impossible, Lord," he prayed. "There are just too many unemployed machinists for one little town. Please help me find an answer."

As he waited quietly for God's answer, the phone rang. Ralph, a former co-worker, told him of a great opportunity to learn a new skill—computer drafting. "They pay you even while you're in training," he said.

Does your situation seem impossible? Take a few moments to ask God for His help.

> MY JOB IS TO TAKE CARE OF THE POSSIBLE
> AND TRUST GOD WITH THE IMPOSSIBLE.

Dear friends, let us love one another, for love comes from God. Everyone who loves has been born of God and knows God.

1 JOHN 4:7 NIV

Love your neighbor as yourself.

MATTHEW 22:39 NIV

My prayer for you is that you will overflow more and more with love for others.

PHILIPPIANS 1:9 TLB

EACH PRECIOUS MOMENT

There are a few moments in life when everything seems perfect—when the list for the school play is posted, and your name is across from the lead role. Then there's that time when you realize your lab partner thinks you're oh-so-much-more-beautiful than the crystalline formations at the bottom of the test tube.

How about the split-second realization that the most wonderful person in the world is now officially your spouse? Or those "are you sure this is my child?" moments that come at just the right time to brighten an otherwise overcast day?

But the best moments always seem to have something to do with love: the love of a friend, a spouse, a child, and God's love. That's because true love is something much greater than we are. It's a taste of the eternal. And those perfect moments? They're a glimpse of the paradise we were created for.

WHERE LOVE REIGNS, THE VERY JOY OF
HEAVEN ITSELF IS FELT.

ACKNOWLEDGEMENTS

Corrie ten Boom (13), Charles Haddon Spurgeon (15), Welsh Proverb (17), Bertha Munro (19), Richard Clarke Cabot (21), Bill Gothard (27), Robert Browning (29), Hannah More (31), William Arthur Ward (41), E. Stanley Jones (43), William Barclay (47), George Herbert (49), Billy Graham (51), Edward McKendree Bounds (53), Henry Van Dyke (55), Charles Swindoll (59), Corrie Ten Boom (61), C.S. Lewis (63), Charles Haddon Spurgeon (65), Hebrew Proverb (67), Robert Harold Schuller (69), Harry Emerson Fosdick (71), Mahatma Gandhi (75), Charles Kingsley (79), Bertha Munro (81), Algernon Charles Swinburne (83), Oswald Chambers (85), F. B. Meyer (87), Jean De La Fontaine (89), Adam Clarke (91), Thomas Aquinas (93), Ralph Waldo Emerson (95), Saint Francis of Sales (99), George Mueller (125), Robert Louis Stevenson (129), Soren Kierkegaard (137), Dwight L. Moody (141), James Moffatt (143), Epicurus (147), Aldous Huxley (153), French Proverb (155), Ralph Waldo Emerson (157), Ian Maclaren (159), Abraham Lincoln (161), Epictetus (163), Robert Browning (165), Euripides (167), Cervantes (169), Cicero (171), Charles R. Swindoll (175), Billy Graham (177), Anthony of Egypt (179), The Cloud of Unknowing (1370) (181), Publilius Syrus (183), Horace Bushnell (185), Lord Alfred Tennyson (187), Sir William Osier (189), Bill Gothard (191), Thomas Dreier (195), Charles L. Allen (197), Augustine of Hippo (199), Izaak Walton (201), Immanuel Kant (203), Geoffrey Chaucer (205), Hannah Hurnard (207).

Additional copies of this book and other titles from Honor Books are available from your local bookstore.

Glimpses of an Invisible God - for Women

Glimpses of an Invisible God - for Mothers

Glimpses of an Invisible God - for Teachers

Glimpses of an Invisible God - for Teens